DAYS OF YORE

A history of Masham and district

compiled by

Susan Cunliffe-Lister

First Published in 1989 by Susan Cunliffe-Lister

Republished 1999
by
WILTON 65
Flat Top House, Bishop Wilton, York. YO42 1RY

ISBN 0 947828 72 9

PRINTED & BOUND BY WILTON 65

Contents

List of Illustrations

Cover design by David Scott

DAYS OF YORE

In memory of the 1st Earl and Countess of Swinton

Acknowledgements

I would like to thank the following: the late Mr A. Wynn for his contribution, Mr Tom Pearson for allowing me to use some extracts from his notes on farming during this century, Mr Jack Musgrave for the loan of many old photographs, Mr George Hare for copying many old photographs, Mrs D. Holland and Mrs K Bradford for much information and memories of the early part of the century, Mr C. Dibnah for help in investigating the Roman period, Mrs Rena Taylor for editing, and Mr Allan Rayden for the photography. I would also like to thank the following for their help with the loan of material or information: Mrs S. Astwood, Mr A. Ayres, Dr J. Anderton, Mr P. Barlow, Mr and Mrs Stuart Blades, Mrs Bumstead, Mr and Mrs C. Carter, County Archivist, Mr Dent, Mr F. Driver, Miss B. Ebsworth, Mr and Mrs W. Edgar, Miss M. Glew, Mr H. Hardy, Mr H. I'Anson, Miss V. Johnson, Mrs J. Johnson, Miss A. Jackson, Mr K. Mallaby, Mrs J. Parratt, Mrs M. Pickard, Mrs J. Prentice, Mr T. Proud, Mr J. Reddington, Mr J. Smith, Mrs Sparkes, Mr J. Thirlwell, Mr H. Tiffney, Mr M. Stanton, Mr H. Ward, Mr F. Wilkinson, Mr E. Wilkinson, Mr T. Theakson, Miss I. Verity, Mrs M. Wood, Mr Toase, Yorkshire Archaeological Society.

I am grateful to the following for permission to reproduce material which is their copyright: Courtauld Institute of Art (University of London), The Fine Art Society Ltd., Country Life, The National Portrait Gallery, and British Rail.

Introduction

I started to write this book with the idea of giving children a picture of how the countryside around them had changed over the years and of the people who lived and worked here through the centuries. I feel it makes history become more alive if you can relate it to familiar places—the fact that the Romans built a road past your house or that the Normans built the church tower make these names from history books seem more real. However as I researched I found a fascinating collection of facts, illustrations and anecdotes which I have compiled into a story which I hope will be of interest to all those who like to know what happened in the 'Days of Yore'.

The Manor of Mashamshire stretches from the banks of the river Yore (now known as Ure) on the east up into the moors on the west. The town of Masham is on the riverside and the villages are spread out between it and the moors. The scenery changes from the fertile river valley to the rugged moorland. The river Yore was named 'Urus' by the Romans which was turned to 'Jore' by the Saxons and to 'Yore' by the Danes. The Normans added 'vallis' to name the valley thus giving 'Jervaulx' abbey its name. Although nowadays the river loses its name when it joins up with the Swale and Ouse there can be little doubt that in ancient times it kept its name as far as York which was called 'Jorvik' by the Danes and pronounced 'Yorvik'—hence the present form York and Yorkshire. For each century I have filled in an outline map of the district showing how the landscape developed—these are only to give a general idea and obviously cannot be accurate in every detail.

1 Early Britons

Writing a local history is rather like being a detective, you have to search for clues and piece them together. The earliest clues we find in the history of Mashamshire are the three earthen circles at Thornborough which are thought to have been in use about 1500 BC during the Bronze Age, possibly for religious rites. Their size suggests that they served more than just the local population and as they lie within five miles of Masham people from this district were sure to have worshipped there. It is now also believed that the temples of standing stones were used by the Bronze Age people rather than by the Druids of a later date. There are three fields behind Fearby called 'standing stones',[1] and although there are no traces now it is possible that this may have been the site of one of these temples. Mr Fisher in his *History of Mashamshire* of 1865 talks of circles of upright stones having recently existed near to Healey.

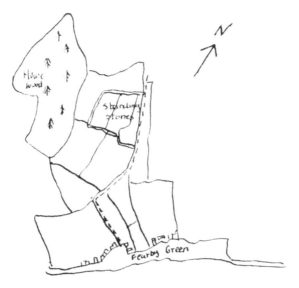

Sketch map showing the position of fields named Standing Stones

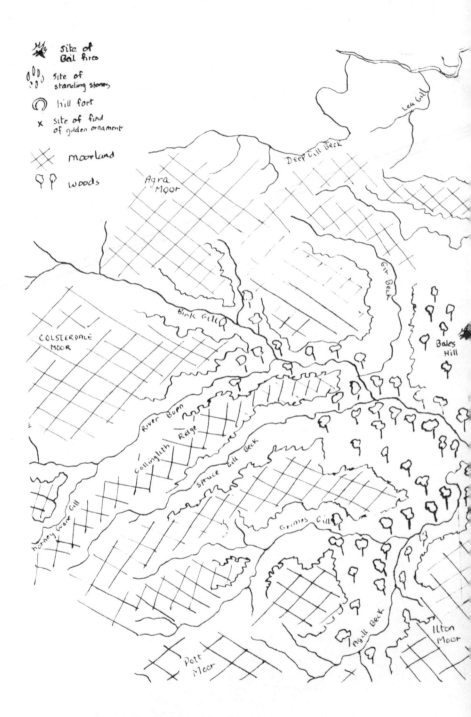

Site of
Bail fires

Site of
standing stones

hill fort

site of find
of golden ornament

moorland

woods

Lea Gill

Deep Gill Beck

Agra Moor

Gir Beck

Bink Gill

Bales Hill

COLSTERDALE MOOR

River Burn

Collingleth Ridge

Spruce Gill Beck

Grimes Gill

Horney Grove Gill

Ingill Beck

Ilton Moor

Pott Moor

River Yore

N

River Yore

Swinney Beck

River Burn

Burn

Den Beck

Sole Beck

Filler Beck

River Yore

Outline map of the district during the time of the early Britons

3

The early Britons of the Bronze Age lived in small huts or shelters made of sticks with stone foundations. They had plots of land that they cultivated by hoeing. Most of their food would have come from hunting wild animals and gathering wild fruits.

In about 100 BC Celtic invaders came from the Continent. They used horsedrawn chariots and made implements from iron including swords. They gradually taught the native Britons their skills and in the Pennines they were formed into a tribal group called Brigantes. They were ruled over by princes and had a number of quite large settlements as well as hill forts and villages. The earthworks at Horsecourse Hill on the edge of Nutwith wood are thought to have originally been the site of a hilltop fort. There are also traces of a village in the fields below Nutwith Common wood and it is probable that the inhabitants used the safety of the fort for themselves and their stock if there was any danger of an attack from a rival group. There would have been other small settlements in the district but their sites have not yet been traced. The climate then was colder and wetter than now and most of the valleys were swampy and thickly wooded and the villages were mostly on the drier hillside. They consisted of circles of huts and a number of irregular fields.

In the Iron Age only the richer people used iron as it was still expensive and everyday tools would have been made of bone and flint. The ordinary people would have been very poor and lived under hard conditions. (A scatter of flint flakes was found in a dry watercourse at Grey Ridge on Pott Moor).[2] They knew how to spin wool and weave cloth and would have been able to make themselves rough clothing.

The escarpment on one side of the hilltop fort at Horsecourse Hill

Druids gathering mistletoe, drawn by David Scott

A golden ornament which was made at this time was found when workmen were digging a sunken fence opposite the entrance gate at Swinton.[3] No one is quite sure what it was used for, some say armlets and others that it was a clasp for a mantle. They might have been sacred ornaments used in religious rites. The Celts worshipped a number of gods. Their priests were called Druids and although some of their religious rites involved human sacrifices they are also thought to have been very wise men who had great influence on the lives of these early people.

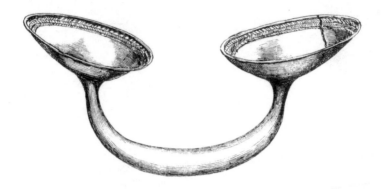

The golden ornament found opposite the entrance gate at Swinton

It is possible that one of the gods worshipped by the Celtic Britons was a Mother Goddess called Bel.[4] There was an old Celtic feast on May 1 when Bel- or Bail-fires were lit on hilltops, and some of the ceremonies connected with the festival are thought to have originated from fertility rites in honour of a Mother Goddess of earlier times. Mr Fisher talks of these Bail-fires and feasts as having continued until recent times in the district—especially in Nidderdale—and that the remembrance of them is transmitted still in the annual feast held at Healey. Bales Hill stands just behind Healey and is the probable site of these ceremonies.

2 Romans

Roman soldiers (from Trajan's column)

In the first century AD the Romans came to England and having conquered the South began to move North. At this time the Brigantes were ruled by a Queen Caritmandus and when one of the native leaders from the South fled to her kingdom she, wanting to keep on friendly terms with the Romans, handed him over to them. Her husband Venutius, a native Brigantian leader, did not like her friendship with the Romans and he led a revolt against her. The Romans helped her in fighting off these attacks for a number of years but eventually she was forced to accept Roman protection in their town of Aldborough. Meanwhile Venutius gathered the Brigantes together and they started to build great defences at Stanwick, 5 km (8 miles) north of Richmond. This must have needed a vast army of workers and they would have come from great distances, including this area, to help. In AD 74, before the building was completed, the Romans attacked and defeated them. The prisoners they took would either have been put to work in building forts and roads to control the natives or sent to serve as soldiers in other countries conquered by the Romans. They were also used to work lead mines of which the Romans had quite a number in the Pennines.

In Mashamshire there have been and still are a number of traces of the Roman presence though few of these have been officially recorded or recognised. Mr Fisher talks of a road running from Kilgram Bridge past Ellington and Marfield westward of Masham and eastward of Swinton to Nutwith and then south to Ripley. From Nutwith he says a road crossed the river to Aldburgh and then eastwards past Well. He also talks of a small oval camp at Swinton and a similar one in Colsterdale. The road from Kilgram Bridge to Nutwith was shown on the Warburton map of Roman roads 1720, and a note on the Overton map of 1728 indicates this road was 7 m (8 yards) wide and paved. These traces may have been more obvious in the 1860s when Mr Fisher wrote his book, but as he offered no evidence then and no one else has since, they have not been recorded on any present-day maps of Roman roads.

I have walked the possible route of the road from Kilgram to Nutwith and the following are the strip maps and observations I have made on it (see illustration on facing page).

From Roomer the road goes down between two hills. At A1 recent ditching in the plantation shows a width of 7 m (8 yards) where the ditch runs under a stone culvert. At A2 there is a bridge over Den Beck with a hollow beside it which might have been a quarry. At A3 there is a terrace down Dykes Hill. At B1 there is another crossing of a stream. This is now the width of the gate but there are signs on both sides that this was once wider. At B2 there are signs of ridges, terracing and paving in the wood. At C1 there is a lot of stone in the hedge as well as smaller stones in the plough on the top of this hill. This is a probable sighting point. At C2 there are traces of stone in the field. From A1 to C2 the land is well cultivated, and from the coming of the Saxons and the establishment of Masham would have been unused; traces are therefore few. From C2 to Kilgram Bridge the terrain is hillier and is not cultivated, it has also continued to be used as a lane and traces are therefore easier to find. One of the things that particularly struck me along this stretch was that most of the gateposts were made of large stone slabs. At D1 there is a distinct ridge on the line of the road. At D2 the lane runs on the site of the road, but at D3 the lane is more of a hollow way and it is likely that it runs along the side of the road. At D4 there is a ridge on the line of the road. From D4 the lane leaves the line of the road but there are signs of terracing between D4 and D5 round the side of the hill. At D5 there is a bridge of large stone flags over a stream. At D6 the stream has been redirected to run westward and there are a great many stones on each bank at the stretch where the road would have crossed. From here the road turns eastward between the two streams to cross the second stream where the present track is and from there it continues on a parallel line to the previous stretch following the line of the present track. The track branches off to the farm and the line of the road continues to Kilgram Bridge.

Many of these traces seem to be at the crossings of small streams. These are where the road surface is least likely to have been disturbed for cultivation and as they are only small streams the force of water will not have washed them away in the same way as in the larger rivers.

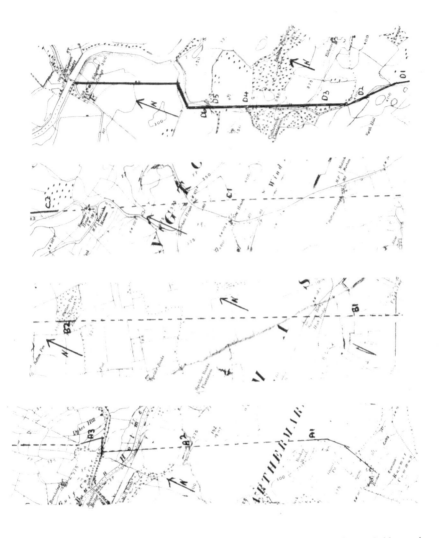

Strip maps showing the possible route of the Roman road between Kilgram bridge and Roomer Common

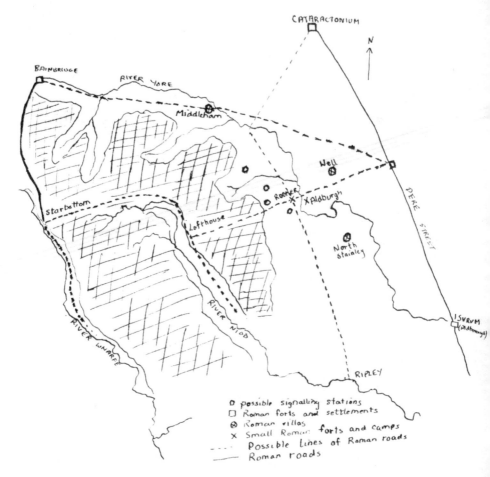

Sketch map of possible lines of Roman roads and tracks

The line of the road from Nutwith crossing the river at Aldburgh probably goes to the Roman settlement near Carthorpe. If this line is continued westward from Nutwith it follows the road across Ilton Moor towards Lofthouse. If you follow it up the edge of Nidderdale and between Great and Little Whernside you eventually come to Starbottom in Wharfedale to where a Roman road from Bainbridge has been traced.[1] I feel this track may have been in use before the Romans came and have led to the hilltop fort at Horsecourse Hill. The Romans probably made use of this track as a crossing of the Pennines. There have been two interesting finds along this route. One was the body of a Roman which was dug up on Grewelthorpe Moor in 1850.[2] It had been preserved in the peat and was tanned, dried and fully clothed in a green cloak, a scarlet garment, yellow stockings and leather sandals. The other was two bronze vessels which the Romans probably used for cooking. These were found at Roundhill in Arnagill.[3]

A flat-topped hill between the camp on Roomer and the river crossing at Nutwith—the reason for its construction is not yet known but I feel it belongs to this period

Roman vessels found at Roundhill in Arnagill

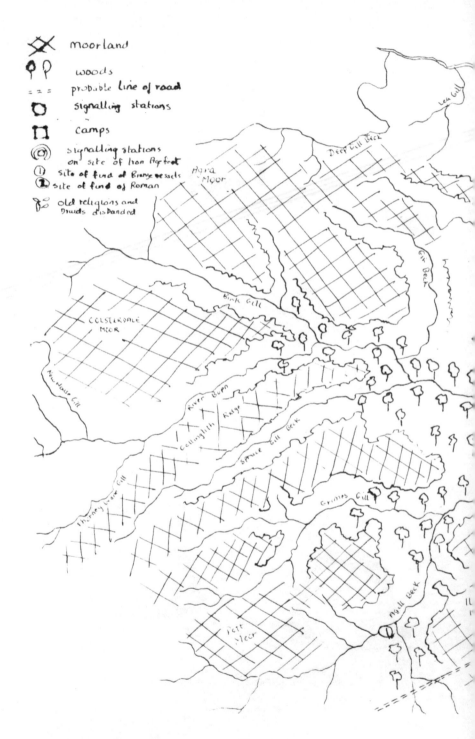

Legend

- ✕ moorland
- ♀♀ woods
- ═ ═ ═ probable line of road
- ⬭ signalling stations
- ⊓ camps
- ◎ signalling stations on site of Iron Age fort
- ① site of find of Bronze vessels
- ② site of find of Roman
- old religions and Druids disbanded

Agra Moor

Lea Gill

Deer Gill Beck

Gill Beck

Black Gill

COLSTERDALE MOOR

New House Gill

River Burn

Collingsith Ridge

Thorney Grane Gill

Spruce Gill Beck

Grimes Gill

Pott Moor

Agill Beck

12

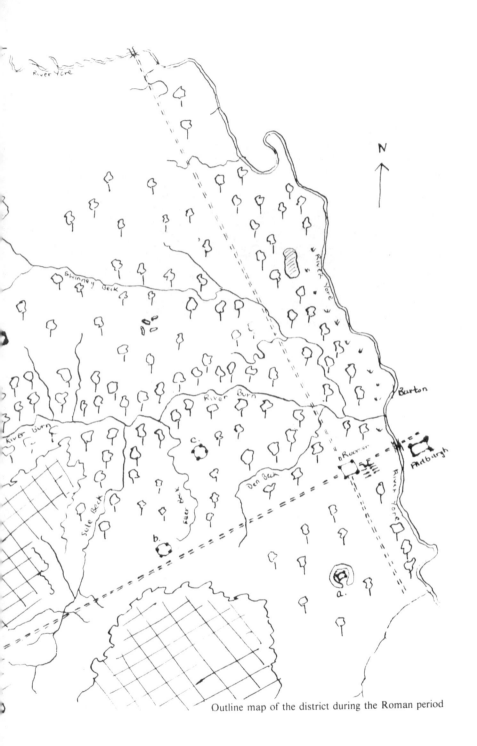

River Yore

Swinney Beck

River Yore

River Burn

Burton

River Burn

c.

n Roman

Sule Beck

Den Beck

Filer Beck

Aldburgh

River Yore

b.

a.

N

Outline map of the district during the Roman period

Aerial view of the camp on Roomer Common

As far as the camps go, the one on Roomer is quite easily discernible and was most probably a small marching camp. There is thought to have been a fort at Aldburgh. The name means 'old fortification' and the name Burton means 'farm beside the fort'. There are still traces of where it is thought to have been but these have not been investigated or recorded. A number of Roman tiles have been discovered in the vicinity during ploughing.

There are another four earthworks of possible Roman origin in the area which are as follows:

(a) Horsecourse Hill—the site of the Iron Age fort. This shows signs of Romanisation and was probably taken over by the Romans. It occupies a very prominent position. A Roman statue was found in an adjoining field SE225774 during ploughing.[4]

(b) A ditched enclosure at 197777 above Ilton which has been identified from aerial photography. This is in a field listed in 1800 as Camp Close[5] and is on the line of the track from Nutwith to Lofthouse.

(c) Swinton 201795 which has again been identified from aerial photography. This is most probably the oval camp which Mr Fisher talks of. The field it is in is listed in 1800 as Tellegraph Field.[6] This was in the days before the telegraph as we know it was invented and then meant 'to signal'. The village beside it is called Warthermarske which means 'Marsh below the watch hill'.[7]

(d) The camp in Colsterdale which Mr Fisher talks of as being similar to the one at Swinton. This has not yet been identified from aerial photography but was most probably on Bales Hill and may either have been planted over or dug out by the potteries which were there later.

14

These earthworks are all so placed as to be visible from one to the other and I feel are part of a series of signalling stations which probably continued south to Aldborough and north via Tranmire to Middleham and either up Wensleydale to Bainbridge or continued north up the edge of the hills.

The duties of the soldiers in a fort were mainly patrolling the part of the road they were in charge of and giving shelter to the numerous travellers. They also had to do regular training and exercises. As the Romans went north into Scotland many of their soldiers were taken from this area and the Brigantes took this chance to break out in revolt. However they were defeated and with peace restored a prosperous period followed. In a town such as Aldborough the Romans had bath-houses with tiles and decorated floors as well as heating systems. Villas such as those at Well and North Stainley were built in the better farming land.

Towards the end of the fourth century, as well as trouble with the Northerners the Romans also had to contend with attacks on the East coast from the Saxons.

3 Saxons

In AD 400 there was trouble on the Continent and the Roman soldiers were called back to defend Rome. The Britons were left on their own to fight off the Saxons and Angles. It was during the period of these fierce attacks that a legendary figure called Arthur came into being. He commanded a small army of horsemen and when a village was being attacked he would often appear from the forest to fight off the invaders. He moved around the country to wherever his help was most needed, and his appearance must have seemed magical to the poor villagers who were being attacked. He was later made into a literary hero, converted into a king and his followers into knights. A local legend tells that Arthur and his knights lie sleeping in a cave under Richmond Castle and when his help is really needed someone will find the entrance to the cave, draw the sword Excalibur and blow the bugle to awaken Arthur and his knights.

The Britons, however, were eventually defeated and Britain was divided into Saxon kingdoms. Yorkshire came into the Saxon kingdom of Northumbria which was ruled over in 617 by King Edwin. King Edwin's wife Queen Ethelburga was a Christian and had a chaplain called Paulinus. He converted King Edwin and travelled round with the court preaching and converting many people. It is said that he baptised more than 10 000 men in the Swale one Christmas Day. King Edwin had a hunting lodge near Tanfield and it is very probable that when Paulinus was there he preached and baptised people from Masham. They then built a church in Masham which would have been paid for by the Saxon lord of the place.[1] Some of the carved stones from this original church were used to rebuild it after it had been burnt. The base of the old Saxon cross now stands outside the door of the church.

The Saxons did not like living in large towns and the ones built by the Romans were soon deserted. They preferred to live in small family groups in clearings in the forests, and villages with names ending in 'ley' and 'ham' are the sites of these early settlements, such as Healey and Masham. These small communities would have had common field agriculture and pastures for the cattle with pigs grazing in the woods. Hamlets such as Masham were usually set on river terraces above the swamp of the river floodplain with a field cleared both up and downstream of the hamlet. Much of their food would still have come from hunting and gathering wild fruits. They used wood for fuel, housebuilding and fences. As the population of these villages increased families from them, and later settlers, established new settlements round about ending in 'ton' (farm), such as Swinton (pig farm), Ilton (Ylca's farm), Ellington (Ella's farm), Sutton (south farm).[2] These settlements soon built up into villages but were in scrubby land, while the 'ley' villages were in thicker woodland.

Saxons, drawn by David Scott

Part of a Saxon cross found in a wall near Masham church

Base of the old Saxon cross now standing in Masham churchyard

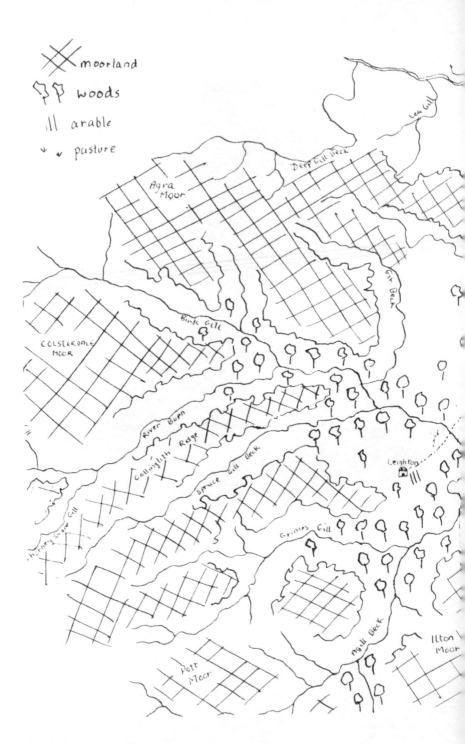

moorland

woods

arable

pasture

Lea Gill

Deep Gill Beck

Agra Moor

Gill Beck

Birk Gill

COLSTERDALE MOOR

River Burn

Collinglith Ridge

Spruce Gill Beck

Leighton

Grimes Gill

Hurney Carr Gill

Ngill Beck

Ilton Moor

Pott Moor

20

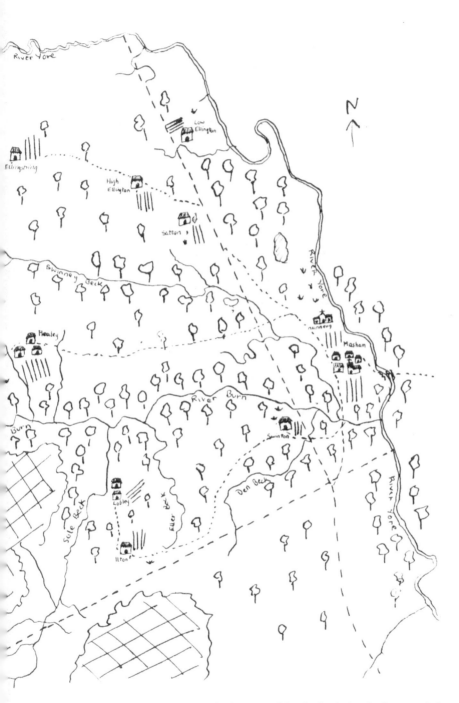

Outline map of the district during the Saxon period

21

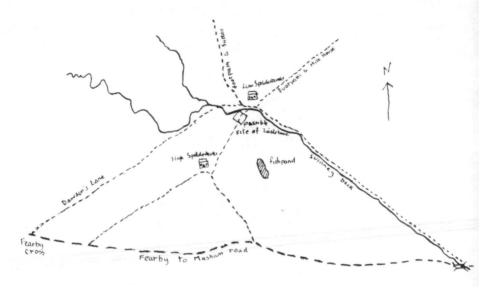

Sketch map of the possible site of Tuiselbroc

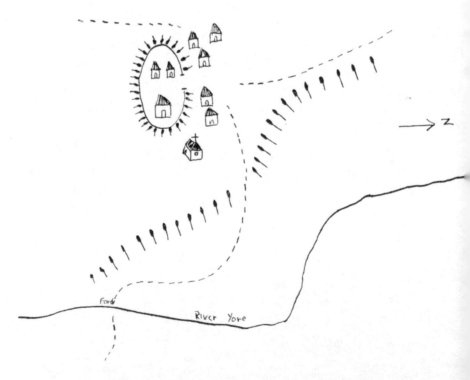

Sketch map showing the early development of Masham

22

Lynchets on the hill above Lobley Hall

I have marked Lobley on the map as a village in Saxon times. Its name indicates that it was one of the early Saxon villages though this name may have been adopted later. However there are traces of lynchets (ancient terraces) on the hill above it and the fact that Lobley Hall remained as the manor house for the manor of Ilton may mean that it was the 'mother' village for Ilton, which is otherwise rather cut off from the other Saxon settlements.

Many of these early villages had fishponds and those at Sutton remain as very good examples. Fish were kept in these to provide fresh food in the winter. There are also ponds at High Mains Whin which may have been the fishponds for Sywardthorpe and Low Ellington. There is one at Spelderbanks which may have been at the site of the village of Tuiselbroc which existed at this time. There is no record of the exact site of this village but it is said to have been near Sutton and Swinton. The name Tuiselbroc means 'fork where two streams meet'[3] and this would apply at Spelderbanks. It is also the junction of no less than five footpaths.

In trying to trace the early development of the hamlet of Masham our main clue is the position of the church. We know that the Saxon church was on the same site. It was usual for the Saxon lords to build churches beside their own enclosures. Gregory Hill (the name Gregory means 'watcher') which lies beside the church, although a natural hill, shows signs of scarpment on the church end which is the only part that has not subsequently been built over. It is possible that the Saxon lord lived in a fortified enclosure on top of the hill. The early markets took place at the entrance to the Lord's enclosure and further houses would have been built around its gates. The old road down Millgate and across the field past the present sewage works leads to the ford which, until the wooden bridge was built at the present site about 1500, was the main crossing place over the river. During the building of the sewage works some old timber was found which dated back to about this time and it is possible that there was a bridge there at some time which was subsequently washed away.

Two stone coffins were dug up at Marfield,[4] in the 1830s, by some workmen digging for gravel in a ridge some 3 to 3½ m (10 to 12 feet) high 180 m (200 yards) from the river bank and near to the Nunneries. These were made from stone which came from Agra rather than Ellington. One of them contained some bones which were thought by the doctor who examined them to be those of a woman. The other was empty.

Because of their situation as well as the fact that one of them contained the skeleton of a woman I feel they are more likely to have been connected with the Saxon Nunnery than with the Romans. Mr Fisher also tells us that a similar one was dug up in Masham but reburied.

Two stone coffins found in Marfield

4 Danes and Norsemen

A 'Northman'

Next came the Danes and Norsemen in their long boats. They landed on the coast and sailed up the rivers attacking the Saxons and Angles and settling where they could. They sailed up the Yore as far as Ripon and it is said that a great battle took place between the Saxons and Danes at Mowbray Wath. Masham suffered a great deal under these attacks as the Danes did not believe in God and took great pleasure in burning churches and destroying any existing buildings. The Saxon church was probably laid waste by the Danes as well as the Nunnery which is said to have existed at Marfield.[1]

Gradually they made peace and the Danes settled in areas so far uninhabited by the Saxons. The names of their settlements ended in 'by' and 'thorpe', such as Fearby (four farms), and Sywardthorpe—this village was near Sutton and was probably one of the seats of Syward, the great and powerful Earl of Northumberland during the reign of Edward the Confessor.[2] At this time the Lord of Masham town was also a Dane called Gospatric.[3]

About AD 900 Norsemen came over the Pennines from Ireland. They came peacefully and as they were mostly sheep farmers they settled on the high land which was not inhabited by the Saxons and Danes. They named their farms 'hus' or house. Beck, gill, mere, ling and side are other Norse names which are much used in this district. They kept their sheep in the valleys during the winter and took them up the hillsides during the summer. This is probably why Summerside at Moorheads was so named. Many of our moorside farms are called '. . . House' and some would have been the sites of these early sheep farms.

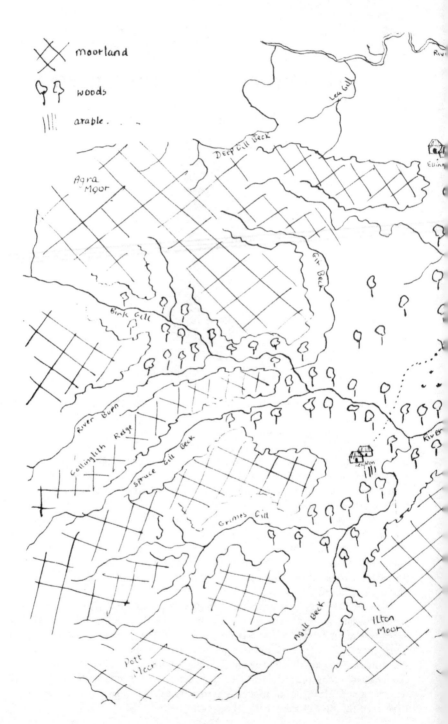

moorland

woods

arable.

Agra Moor

Deep Gill Beck

Lea Gill

Riv

Ellin

Gill Beck

Birk Gill

River Burn

Collinglith Ridge

Spruce Gill Beck

River

...ton

Grimes Gill

River

Agill Beck

Ilton Moor

Pott Moor

26

Outline map of the district showing changes brought by the Danes

27

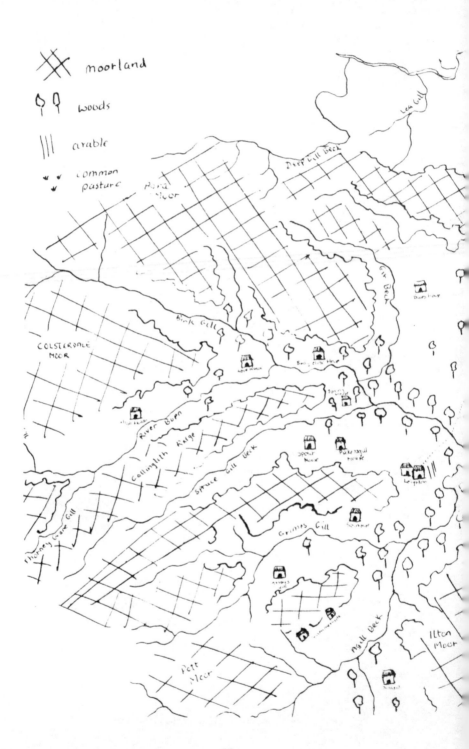

moorland

woods

arable

common pasture

Lea Gill

Deep Gill Beck

Pura Moor

Gill Beck

Dovis Hour

Birk Gill

COLSTERDALE MOOR

Bails Cliff Hour

River Burn

Collinglith Ridge

Spout Moor

Picke Gesgill House

Knighton

Spruce Gill Beck

Thorney Grane Gill

Grimes Gill

Agill Beck

Ilton Moor

Pott Moor

28

Outline map of the district showing possible sites of early Norsemen settlements

5 Normans

Norman soldiers

Masham had scarcely recovered from the attacks of the Danes before it had to undergo even worse trials. Edward the Confessor, the last of the Saxon kings died in 1066 and the English nobles chose Harold as their King. However William, Duke of Normandy, also claimed the throne and landed in England at the head of a large army. He defeated Harold at the battle of Hastings in 1066 and became King of England. William then marched round the country taking land from the Saxons and Danes and giving it instead to his Norman followers.

Two of the Saxon lords from the North who threatened to cause William most trouble were Earl Edwin, who was Lord of Mashamshire, and his brother Morcar, who was Lord of Ilton. At first William, keen to gain the support of two such powerful lords, gave them important jobs at his coronation and promised that Earl Edwin should marry one of his daughters. They therefore gave him their support but later when Edwin asked when the marriage was to take place William insulted them. They secretly left the Norman court and joined the other northern lords at York to fight William. Gospatric, the lord of Masham town, also joined them and there was a long siege. In the end the Saxons were defeated by famine and Morcar was taken prisoner by the Normans. Edwin made secret plans to release his brother but he was betrayed by his own followers and killed by some Norman soldiers. His death was much regretted not only by his own countrymen but by the Norman lords as well as he had been a good and brave lord. William was so upset when he heard about it that he banished the soldiers who had killed him.[1]

After he had defeated the Saxons at York, William marched north making his soldiers burn the villages and drive away the cows and pigs. Mashamshire suffered a great deal as we can see from the entries in the Domesday Book. This was a list of the number of people and the amount of cultivated land etc. in all the villages which William had made. These were the entries for Mashamshire:

Yorkshire—the land of Earl Alan

In Ellintone to be taxed six carucates and there may be four ploughs. Gospatric (two carucates) and Norman (three carucates and two oxgangs), and Torchil (six oxgangs) had three manors there. The same Gospatric now has what he had, of the Earl. In the demesne one plough, and three bordars with one plough. In the rest of the land the Earl has six villanes, with three ploughs. Meadow six acres. The whole one mile and a half long and half a mile broad. Value in King Edward's time forty shillings, now thirty shillings.

In Siwarthorp to be taxed one carucate, and there may be one plough. A moiety of this is in land of Masham. Torchil had it, now the Earl, and it is waste.

In Sutton to be taxed one carucate, and there may be one plough. Norman had a Manor there. Earl Alan now has it, and it is waste. The whole half a mile long and half broad. Value in King Edward's time ten shillings.

In Fearby to be taxed three carucates, and there may be two ploughs. Gospatric and Eldred had there two manors. The Earl has them now, and Gospatric of him. Eight villanes and one bordar have there two ploughs and a half. The whole half a mile long and four quarantens broad. Value in King Edward's time, ten shillings, now sixteen shillings.

In Ilton to be taxed two carucates, and there may be two ploughs. Archil had a manor there. Gospatric has now there one plough and three villanes and two bordars. The whole half a mile long and half broad. Value in King Edward's time, sixteen shillings, now eight shillings.

In Masham to be taxed twelve carucates, and there may be eight ploughs. Gospatric had there one manor. Ernegis has now there one plough, and ten villanes and three bordars with five ploughs. There is a church.

To this manor belong the berewicks—Tuiselbroc, three carucates; Swinton three carucates and a half; and Sutton, one carucate—to be taxed seven carucates and a half, and there may be four ploughs. They are waste. The whole manor, with the berewicks, one mile long and one broad. Value in King Edward's time, six pounds, now sixteen shillings.

A *bordar* was a person who held a cottage and small parcel of land and had to supply the lord with poultry, eggs and etc.

A *villane* (or villein) held land by a servile tenure—as a slave.

A *carucate* was as much land as one team of oxen could plough in a year—it varied between 48 to 72 hectares (120 to 180 acres).

A survey done in 1183 is the last mention we have of the villages of Siwardthorpe and Tuiselbroc.

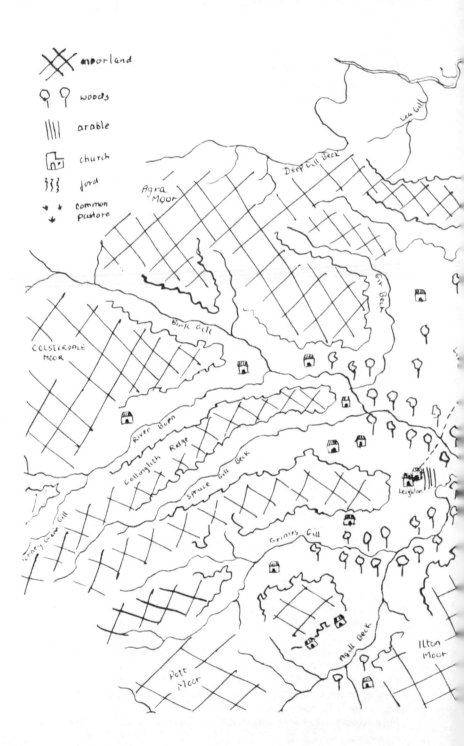

moorland
woods
arable
church
ford
common pasture

Lea Gill

Deep Gill Beck

Agra Moor

Gill Beck

Birk Gill

COLSTERDALE MOOR

River Burn

Collinglith Ridge

Spruce Gill Beck

Leighton

Grimes Gill

Pott Moor

Agill Beck

Ilton Moor

Outline map of the district showing the changes that came about during the Norman Conquest

A vassal paying homage to his lord

When the King gave land to his followers he did it on a feudal basis. This meant he divided the land into Knight's fees and granted these to his followers. Instead of paying rent to the King for the land the lords had to go and fight for him for forty days every year bringing armed men with them—the number of these depended on the amount of land they had been granted. They also had to pay homage to the King as did their followers. These lords in their turn granted some of this land to their friends and family on the same condition of coming to fight for them when required. This land would probably be sublet again a number of times on the same conditions. The King was therefore assured of an army whenever he wanted one and many from Mashamshire were thus involved in the wars of these early centuries.

King William gave all Earl Edwin's land to one of his followers, Earl Alan. It was he who gave the monks of Fountains wood at Burton, probably for building a cell at Aldburgh, common of pasture in Swinton and Roomer and dead wood for making charcoal for their forge. Earl Alan's brother later gave Mashamshire to Nigel de Albini who had been one of the captains in William's army that had laid waste to this part of the country. He later became bow-bearer to King William Rufus and was with the King when he was mysteriously killed by an arrow out hunting in the New Forest. Nigel de Albini was a great warrior and because of his bravery he became very rich and powerful. He was succeeded by his son Roger de Mowbray who was as brave a warrior as his father. When he was still a youth he not only fought at the head of his men from Masham and other lands but he was also one of

34

the commanders of the King's army which won a great victory over the Scots at the Battle of the Standard at Northallerton in 1138. He then went on the Crusades. These were military expeditions, the object of which was to capture the Holy Land from the Mohammedans. On one of these he was taken prisoner by Saladin but he was later redeemed by the Knights Templar.[2]

Roger de Mowbray was a very good Christian and like other feudal lords at this time he gave a lot of his land to monasteries and abbeys. He granted Masham church to the church of St Peter in York, and established it as a prebend. The

The Norman door in the church tower

35

Fallow deer in the park at Swinton

Archbishop of York then freed it from 'all the customs and claims of his archdeacons and officials'. In consequence of this the Peculier Court of Masham (peculier is the Norman French for 'peculiar', meaning particular rather than odd) was established. This was an ecclesiastical court which judged all offences of a religious nature as well as having the power amongst other things to grant probates of wills, licences to curates, schoolmasters and parish clerks and marriage licences. The tower and the west doorway in the church would have been built at this time, possibly at the instigation of Roger de Mowbray, and are good examples of Norman architecture.

At this time we can picture Mashamshire as being a forest with thick woods as well as thinner scrubby woodland. Here and there would be little villages surrounded by patches of cultivated ground. The woods would be full of wild boars, wolves, foxes and wild cats while fallow deer would graze in the more open land. In the forests of Wensleydale there were said to be bears and wild bulls.

One of the important jobs in a village was that of swineherd. Most of the villagers kept pigs and were given permission by the Lord of the district to graze them in the forest. At the end of Masham town on the way to Swinton there is a field called Swine-garth and every morning the swineherd would go there and blow his horn. The people of Masham would then open their piggery doors and the grunting inmates would make their way to Swine-garth. When they were all there the swineherd would take them out to feed in the forest and bring them back to their homes in the evening. The wild boar were also plentiful in this district and were much prized for hunting. Anybody who killed a wild boar without Royal Authority was punished with the loss of his eyes.

We have the first mention of a mill in the district, although there were probably some here previously, when Roger de Mowbray gave a charter to John son of Drin granting him Burton and allowing him to make a mill there.[3]

6 1200

Mashamshire passed from the de Mowbray family to the de Buheres and then to the Wautons. It is probable that the de Wauton family had a manor house in Masham. This may have been on the site of Park House. A house called 'the Old Hall', which indicates a manor house, is named in deeds of 1600 as being sold along with two fields called Paddock Sykes or Paradise.[1] Paradise fields lie directly behind Park House. Possibly the names 'Park Street, Park Square' indicate the siting of a park attached to the manor. This may have taken in the land between Masham and Burnholme which does not seem to have traces of the strip farming of the old open fields nor to have been part of the common fields.

Sketch map showing the development of Masham with the strip fields, common pasture and possible park boundary

A Cistercian monk

We now find the monks from Fountains and Jervaulx Abbeys beginning to make their presence felt in the district. Fountains Abbey was founded in 1132 and Jervaulx in 1145. The monks in both these abbeys were of the Cistercian order. They were very skilled in sheep-breeding and iron-making. This was to stand them in good stead as the land given to the abbeys was usually in the wilder areas; this was certainly the case in Mashamshire where the monks of Jervaulx had a grange in Colsterdale and the monks of Fountains had theirs at Pott. The monks, however, quickly improved the land for breeding their sheep. Fountains Abbey also had granges at Nutwith Cote and Aldburgh, and in 1201 when Gilbert Wauton gave the grange of Pott to Fountains he also gave them the right to make a road from Nutwith to Pott. It seems very probable that the two bridges at Leighton, one under the reservoir and the other at Burgess Bank were part of this road. It is still traceable as far as Broadmires, but whether it went via their mill at Ilton or to Swinton from there it is difficult to say. There were iron mines in Colsterdale, and in 1250 the then Lord of Mashamshire signed a deed saying that he would no longer work the mines or sell them though whether this was so as not to disturb the grange or so that the monks themselves should have sole use of them is debatable.

The monks did a lot of good work, nursing the sick, looking after the poor and teaching young boys. Because of this, and also in exchange for the monks saying prayers for themselves and their families, rich men gave them fields and farms and they gradually came to own a considerable amount. We later find the abbey of Jervaulx owning land at Ellingstring and Ellington and that of Fountains at Ilton and Swinton.

Bridge now under Leighton reservoir photographed during the drought of 1976

Burgess Bank bridge

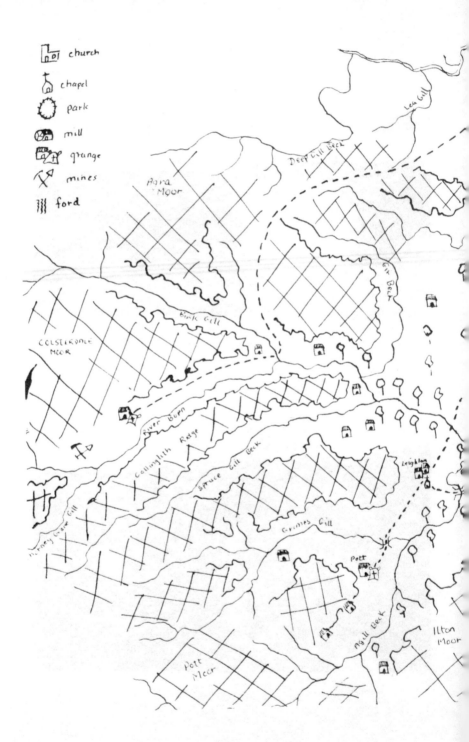

church

chapel

park

mill

grange

mines

ford

Lea Gill

Deer Gill Beck

Agra Moor

Gir Beck

Birk Gill

COLSTERDALE MOOR

River Burn

Collinglith Ridge

Spruce Gill Beck

Nidney Gaw Gill

Grimes Gill

Leighton

Pott

Mill Beck

Ilton Moor

Pott Moor

40

Outline map of the district during the thirteenth century

The Masham breed of sheep

At this time the churches were very rich as everybody had to pay tithes to them. Tithes were a tenth of what they produced in the way of lambs, fleeces, corn and hay, etc. The people of Mashamshire must have been particularly productive probably mostly with their sheep, as Masham prebend was one of the richest in the country—it was worth 250 marks (approx £170) in 1291[2]—and was much sought after by powerful priests who would be given the living. This meant that they took all the money and would send a curate to do the work in the parish and give them so much for the upkeep of the church etc. In 1291 this was 30 marks (approx £20). In the middle of the century the living of Masham church belonged to Roger de Clare who also held the livings of thirteen other churches—neglecting them all. To put this right, in 1278 it was decided by the Dean and Chapter of York that the tithes of Masham should be divided between the prebendary and a vicar. The vicar should live in the parish, the upkeep of which he should be responsible for, while the prebendary should be responsible for the upkeep of the church and be able to appoint a new vicar when necessary. A church was also built at Ellington and was dedicated in 1287: it was a chapel of ease used by the monks of Jervaulx.

There are some old potteries in the district which were probably in existence at this time. There was one on the site of Healey church. The field was known as Potter's field and when the foundations of the church were being excavated many misshapen pots were found. There also appears to have been another pottery at a place on Bales Hill called 'Potter's Pitt' where some claypits have evidently been worked and where, also, misshapen pots have been found. This place was a very ancient enclosure from the moor.[3]

The following is an Inquisition of fees in Richmondshire taken in 1286. NB: a carucate is the amount of land that a team of oxen could plough in a season:

Ilketon   There are three carucates there which are holden of Hugh Fitz Henry: and the same Hugh holdeth of John de Wauton; and the same John, of Roger de Mowbray: and Roger of the Earl: and the Earl of the King.

Swinton   There are six carucates of land there whereof twelve make (a knight's fee) etc.—of which four carucates are holden of Ralph de Normanville: and the same Ralph holdeth the residue of Hugh Fitz Henry: and the same Hugh, of John de Wauton: and John, of the Earl: and the Earl of the King.

Helhe and Sutton   There are in the same Vills there, five carucates of land which are holden of John de Wauton, and the same John of Roger Mowbray: and Roger, of the Earl: and the Earl of the King.

Elynstrynge   There is one carucate of land there—of which the Abbot of Joreval holdeth one bovate of land of Walter le Latryn: and the same Walter holdeth the same bovate and three other bovates of John de Wauton: and the same John holdeth the residue of Roger Mowbray: and the same Roger of the Earl: and the Earl of the King.

Ellyngton   There are six carucates of land there—of which three carucates are holden of John de Wauton: and Abbot of Joreval likewise holdeth of the same John, and renders by the year 10s.; and the same John of Roger Mowbray, and the same Roger of the Earl: and the Earl of the King.

Masham and Little Burton   There are twenty-seven carucates of land in the same Vills, and they answer for one knight's fee: also, there are six carucates of land there—of which the Master of the Knight's Templars in England holdeth two bovates of land in pure alms, and the residue is holden by John de Wauton: and the same John of Roger, Mowbray: and the same Roger of the Earl: and the Earl of the King.

Fearby   There are three carucates of land there which Elias de Fetherby holdeth; two carucates of John de Wauton and the same John of Avice Marmyon: and the same Avice of John Earl of Richmond: and the same Earl of the King: also the aforesaid Elias holdeth one carucate of land of Gilbert de Clifton: and the same Gilbert of the heirs of Thornton Steward: and the same heirs of the Earl: and the Earl of the King.

Burton-on-Yore   There are 4 carucates of land there, whereof 14 etc., which Richard of Great Burton holdeth of Mary de Neville, and the same Mary of the Earl, and the Earl of the King.

7 **1300**

In 1328 the widow of John Wauton sold Mashamshire to Sir Geoffrey de Scrope. He gained great distinction in tournaments and was knighted for his valour. He held the office of King's serjeant to Edward II and was employed by both Edward II and Edward III as a diplomat negotiating matters of state. As a soldier he accompanied Edward II on his invasion of Scotland and Edward III to France. (Edward III claimed to be the rightful King of France which involved England in the Hundred Years War.) His son Sir Henry le Scrope succeeded him. He too was a soldier of great distinction and served in the Scottish wars during the reign of Edward III when a few of the English nobility placed Baliol on the throne of Scotland. During the reign of Richard II he was sent with others to negotiate with Charles, King of Navarre, a treaty between them. He was succeeded by his son Sir Stephen Scrope

King Richard setting out on a crusade

who served in his father's train in the wars of France, became a Crusader and went to the Holy Land. He was summoned to Parliament from 1393 to 1406.

Some of the powerful priests who sought the living of Masham church during this century were the following: William de Ayreman who was one of the surpliced churchmen who fought at the battle of Myton-upon-Swale in 1319 when he was taken prisoner by the Scots. He was made Bishop of Norwich in 1325 and later made Lord Chancellor of England. The next prebendary was John de Ufford. He was made Archbishop of Canterbury by the Pope at the King's request but was never consecrated as he died of the plague. In 1370 Robert de Stratton became prebendary. He was said 'to be a chaplain to the Black Prince, utterly unworthy of so high preferment, being an illiterate fellow'.[1]

There were quite a number of mills in the district by now. There was one at Ilton which the owner Sir Richard de Waxwand allowed the monks of Fountains to use. This would have been very useful to them when they had their cow-grange at Pott. There was also a mill at Swinton which belonged to the monks of Fountains and they had another at their grange at Nutwith. There were two other corn mills in Mashamshire which were valued in 1392 at £10 which was a very great sum in those days. In 1332 there is a deed of sale of some land between Robert de Evesham and Thomas, miller of Masham.[2]

In 1334 Sir Geoffrey le Scrope granted the Abbot and Convent of Jervaulx the sole right of getting coals upon the wastes of Colsterdale for a rent of 8 marks yearly. Coal was not used much in England until after 1600 as it was thought to be unhealthy, but the monks used it for smelting their iron ore.

Tenants had to do certain work for their lords such as ploughing their fields and harvesting their crops etc. in return for their lands. The lords of the various hamlets at this time were as follows:

Masham   Hugh de Hopham
Burton   Roger Cysell
Swinton   Ralph de Normanville
Ilton   John Waxwand, Abbot of Fountains, Master of Magdalen Hospital
Healey   Hugh de Hopham, John de Henton
Fearby   Reginald de Clyfton, John Alward
Ellington with Ellingstring   Abbot of Jervaulx and heirs of Richard Cysell

On the death of Henry le Scrope in 1392 a valuation of Masham was made as follows:

Henry Scrope held the Manor of Masham of Thomas de Mowbray, Earl Marshall by the service of one barbed arrow by the year for all services; and there is in the same manor:

one capital messuage which is worth nothing by the year beyond reprizes,
166 acres of land, every acre is worth 8d a year—110s 8d.
30 acres of meadow, every acre worth 2s a year—60s.
rents of Free tenants—£4 6s 1d.
rent of one pound of Pepper price 14d.
rent of bondmen and tenants at will—£51 8s 1d.
rents of divers tenants for works—77s 3½d.
two water corn mills—£10.
coal mine—40s.
perquisites of Courts—33s 4d.

45

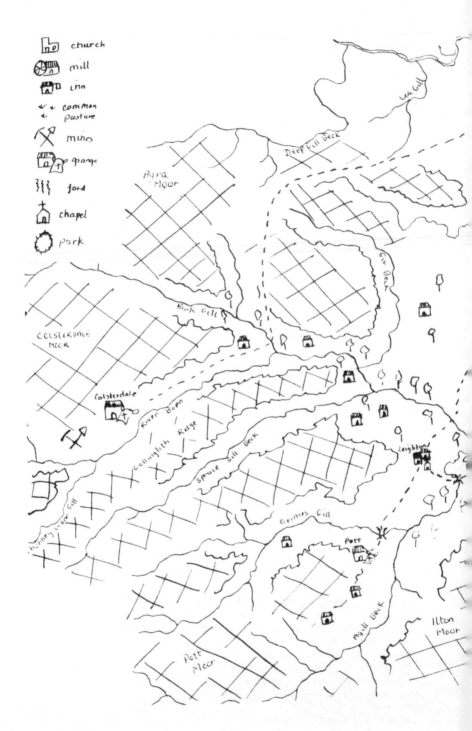

church
mill
inn
common pasture
mines
grange
ford
chapel
park

Lea Gill

Deep Gill Beck

Agra Moor

Gir Beck

Birk Gill

COLSTERDALE MOOR

Colsterdale

River Burn

Collinglith Ridge

Spruce Gill Beck

Horney Carr Gill

Leighton

Grimes Gill

Pott

Pott Moor

Nidd Beck

Ilton Moor

46

Outline map of the district during the fourteenth century

In the 1340s plague swept the country and many people died. Some of the more isolated villages such as Ellingstring escaped. In other villages which suffered there were not enough tenants left to do all the lord's work. As a result some gave up their land and worked full time for wages instead.

Houses of this period were 'crucked'. This consisted of two curved timbers meeting in the middle. These were held together by a cross timber forming a letter A. Two or more of these crucks were put 3 or 3½ m (10 to 12 feet) from each other and held the rooftree. The roof was thatched and a headless barrel was placed in the thatch as an escape hole for the smoke from an open fire in the room below. The walls were timber. The oxen often lived under the same roof.

Some of Low Burton Hall is thought to date from this century though this would have been built of stone.

The Lords of Masham at this time were granted charters to hold markets and fairs in Masham. In 1393 Stephen le Scrope was granted a weekly market on Wednesdays and two fairs yearly to be held on the Feast of St Barnabas the Apostle and on the eve and day of the Assumption of the Blessed Virgin (17 and 18 September). The farmers brought their butter, eggs and cheese to sell at the markets and bought and sold cattle and sheep. The fairs were enlarged markets with all sorts of amusements added. Also they were where the people had to buy all the cloth for making clothes, and household wares they would need until the next fair. The fairs in Masham were very popular as they were free of tolls; the people of Richmond complained that their fairs suffered because of this and their property deteriorated in value. This influx of people created the need for a number of inns and there were many more than there are now. The villages of Swinton and Ilton even had their inns as they were on the main road from Nidderdale. These inns would, no doubt, have done very well as a great deal of intoxicating liquor was drunk in those days.

The old part of Low Burton Hall

The Market Cross in Masham Square

8 1400

Henry Scrope succeeded his father in 1406. He was made Lord Treasurer of England in 1409 by Henry IV. In 1413 Henry V decided to claim the Crown of France, as the heir of Isabella the wife of Edward II, so he sent Henry, Lord Scrope and some others to the Court of Charles VI, King of France, to make his unjust demand. As this was refused Henry V decided to invade France and he ordered all his troops to go to Southampton. He went there himself with Lord Scrope to superintend the embarkation. While they were there a conspiracy to kill the king was discovered and the Earl of Cambridge and Lord Scrope were both arrested, and accused of plotting to kill the king and of intending to proclaim the Earl of March as the rightful king. A number of peers were gathered to try them and they were condemned to death without being given any chance to speak in their own defence. The Earl of Cambridge confessed and accused the Earl of March of agreeing to the plot but at the same time he cleared Henry, Lord Scrope of having anything to do with it. Unfortunately this came too late and when he was beheaded all his lands were taken away; the King later repented this decision and gave them back to his family.

John Scrope succeeded to his father. He was more of a diplomat than a military man. He was appointed High Treasurer of England in 1432. His son Sir Thomas Scrope lived during the Wars of the Roses and supported the House of Lancaster in spite of the fact that most of his neighbours supported the House of York. In 1459 the Queen of Henry VI, wishing to enlist the sympathies of the men of the North on behalf of her child the Prince of Wales, brought him on a trip round the North. Whilst she was doing this the Earl of Salisbury raised an army of 5000 at Middleham (some men from Masham were sure to have been amongst them) and went to fight under the Standard of the White Rose of York and against the King. The result was the battle of Bloreheath which was fought on 23 September 1459 and won by the Lancastrians. The Earls of Warwick, March (afterwards King Edward IV) and Salisbury and other members of the House of York were forced to flee to Calais. As the Lancastrians had won, a few days afterwards Sir Thomas le Scrope, the then Lord of Mashamshire, received the honour of a summons to Parliament as the fifth Lord Scrope of Masham and he was further rewarded with a grant of an annuity of twenty marks for his service against the house of York—a sufficient proof of his devotion and loyalty to his King. These Wars lasted for thirty years and the Yorkists were successful in installing Edward IV as King for twenty-two years. However the House of York was finally overthrown in the battle of Bosworth Field on 22 August 1485 when Richard III (the Duke of Gloucester who imprisoned his nephews Edward V and his brother in the Tower of London—most probably for their own safety—where they were mysteriously murdered) was killed and his army defeated by Henry VII.

Richard III at the Battle of Bosworth

Thomas Scrope was succeeded by his son, another Thomas, who still supported the cause of the red rose. However this does not seem to have prevented him from being summoned to the Parliament of Edward IV and being appointed cup-bearer at the coronation of Richard III.

Soon after his accession to the throne, Henry VII made a trip round the North in 1486 to win over the nobility and gentry to his interests. While he was at Pontefract he learnt that Lord Lovell, formerly chamberlain to Richard III had raised a force of 3000 to 4000 men from the district of Middleham and Ripon (again this would no doubt include a number of men from Masham) and planned to surprise the King on his entry to York. The King sent a messenger to persuade the men to return home and offered them a free pardon if they did so. This did the trick and the army dispersed.

Lord Lovell was forced to flee abroad. However, he had not given up the fight and he was to return shortly to Masham on his way once again to try and unseat Henry VII. Richard III had had another brother as well as Edward IV—this was the Duke of Clarence who was put to death in the Tower of London, but left behind a son, the Earl of Warwick. He was kept imprisoned by Henry VII but the Yorkists found a boy of the same age called Lambert Symnel whom they trained to pretend he was Earl of Warwick. He was taken to Ireland which was very much in favour of the cause of York, and he was there crowned King Edward VI. He was joined by the Earl of Lincoln and Lord Lovell among others and with an army of about 8000 German and Irish troops they landed in Lancashire. They expected that a great many people, dissatisfied with Henry VII, would join them but this did not happen and they quickly made their way through Lancashire and Westmorland to arrive in Masham four days after their landing. They set up their quarters here and sent a message to the Lord Mayor of York asking that the City of York should receive them. However this was refused and a message stating this was delivered to the rebel leaders at Boroughbridge on their way to York. They then changed their route and made for London. They were intercepted at Stoke near Newark by Henry VII's army, led by the Earl of Oxford, and were defeated after a fierce battle lasting about three hours. The Earl of Lincoln was killed and Lord Lovell apparently escaped; he was never seen again and it is thought he was drowned trying to swim his horse across the river Trent. A number of the rebels were hanged in York but Lambert Symnel was given a pardon and made a scullery boy in Henry VII's kitchens.[1]

Remains of the old chapel at High Burton (now destroyed)

Remains of the cross on Fearby green

The abbeys of Fountains and Jervaulx still had a great deal of influence in the district. As well as the chapel of ease at Ellington which was in the care of the monks of Jervaulx, there were chapels at Leighton and Fearby which were in the care of the monks of Fountains. There were also private chapels at High and Low Burton and most probably at the Fountains grange at Aldburgh. The chapel at Leighton was later converted into a farmhouse and the chapel at Fearby was said to have been in a cottage called Chapel House which was recently demolished.

At Fearby Cross there are the remains of an old cross. These crosses used to stand in streets and at road junctions. Sermons used to be preached at them, royal proclamations made, laws published and sometimes even hangings took place. During funerals the procession would stop at them and prayers would be said; this was frowned on after the Reformation, and in 1634 we find someone being brought before the Peculier Court in Masham for doing just this.

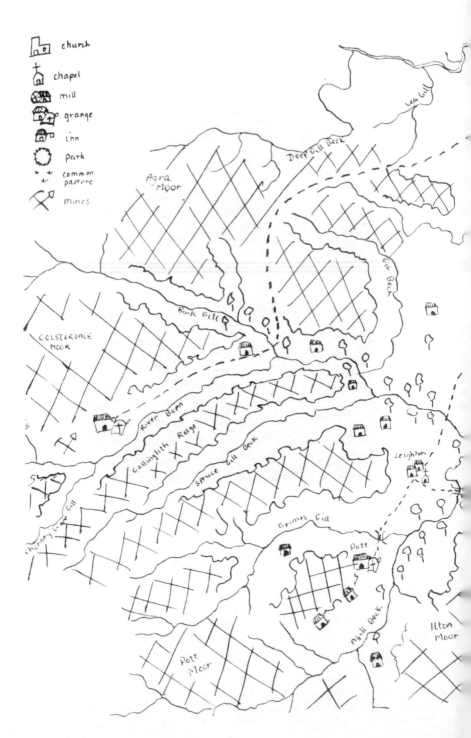

church
chapel
mill
grange
inn
park
common pasture
mines

Lea Gill

Deep Gill Beck

Agra Moor

Gib Beck

Birk Gill

COLSTERDALE MOOR

River Burn

Collingcith Ridge

Spruce Gill Beck

Leighton

Thorney Grane Gill

Grimes Gill

Pott

Ilton Moor

Agill Beck

Pott Moor

54

Outline map of the district during the fifteenth century

Beehives at Nutwith Cote

In 1453 we have the following details concerning the grange at Nutwith which the Beckwiths had for Fountains Abbey:

The rent was 30s a year. They had to keep 20 cows of the stock of the monastery and to return of their annual proceeds:

13st 4lb of butter at 12d a stone,
26st 8lbs of cheese at 8d a stone,
10 stirkettes each to be worth 4s.

The tenant of Nutwith was paid 8d for carrying wool from his house to the Abbey; and a lad was paid 2d for driving a flock of sheep from Fountains to Nutwith.[2]

The beehives at Nutwith probably date from about this time. The family of Beckwith were very prolific and were to take part in many aspects of life in Mashamshire over the years.

A survey done of the land held by the abbeys, after the Reformation, gives us some idea of the size of the granges:

Nutwith—89 acres: 42 acres were arable and meadow and the rest was pasture.
Aldburgh—316 acres: 3 acres arable, 74 meadow, the rest was pasture.
Pott—239 acres: 78 acres meadow, the rest was pasture.
Ashehed—108 acres: 40 acres meadow, the rest was pasture.
Over Ashehed—24 acres: 9 acres meadow, the rest was pasture.
There was also pasture on Come Fell, Pott Moor, and Roomer, there were 6 tenements in Swinton, 5 tenements in Ilton and 1 in Wardenmerske.[3]

Masham church was still much sought after as a living and in 1447 the Earl of Warwick, the most powerful of the Yorkist nobles and known as 'Warwick, the Kingmaker', obtained the prebend for his brother George Neville, aged seven. He did not stay long as he was made Bishop of Exeter when he was about eighteen. The church spire was built above the Norman tower during this century.

More people were leaving the villages and settling in small clearings in the forest, and taking up skills such as thatching, fencing, ditching, and stone-getting rather than spending all their time in producing their own food.

Masham church spire

9 1500

Battle of Flodden Field

In July 1503 Princess Margaret, the eldest daughter of Henry VII, visited Yorkshire on her way to Scotland for her marriage to James IV, King of Scotland. Henry, the seventh Baron Scrope of Masham, was among other members of the nobility and gentry who vied with each other to entertain this beautiful and interesting princess. He little guessed then that he would help to make her a widow a few years later. This happened at the battle of Flodden Field. In 1513, while Henry VIII was in France with his army, James IV of Scotland picked a quarrel with him about some jewels he said should be his. He raised an army and marched South. The Earl of Surrey called upon the Northern counties to arm and Henry, Lord Scrope joined his army at the head of the men of Mashamshire. They took a prominent part in the battle in which King James was killed and the English army proved victorious.

Henry, Lord Scrope, did not long survive the battle and was succeeded by his two brothers Ralph and Geoffrey, but they too did not live long; Geoffrey died in 1517 and the male branch of the house of Scrope of Masham thus died out. The estates were divided between Geoffrey's three sisters Margery Danby, Elizabeth Fitz Randolf of Spennithorne and Alice Strangways of Harsley. Mashamshire went to Margery Danby and thus the Danbys became the new Lords of Mashamshire.

Sir Christopher Danby, husband of Margery, did not long survive his good fortune and was succeeded by his son Christopher who was only fifteen. In spite of his age he was already married to Elizabeth, the third daughter of his neighbour, Richard Neville, second Lord Latimer, who lived at Snape Castle. Her brother, the third Lord Latimer, was the husband of Katharine Parr who became the sixth and last wife of Henry VIII. Her sister married Richard Norton of Norton Conyers, who was the real leader of the Rebellion of 1569 in support of Mary, Queen of Scots (then imprisoned at Bolton Castle) against Elizabeth I.

Difficult times were coming. Henry VIII was becoming bored with his wife Catherine of Aragon and decided he wanted to marry Anne Boleyn. However, the Pope would not allow him to divorce Catherine of Aragon, and so with the help of Cromwell and Cranmer he shook off the authority of the Pope and made himself 'In England the Supreme Head on earth of the church'. This was the Reformation, but for some a reformation it certainly was not. If he had done no more, things would

Henry VIII by an unknown artist (National Portrait Gallery)

59

The ruins of Jervaulx Abbey

not have been too bad but he was very short of money, so he decided to plunder the churches. Christopher Danby, along with the rest of the people of Masham, had to watch the King's men take possession of their church and chapels and disband the monastries of Fountains and Jervaulx, seizing their granges. The monks were sent out into the world to seek a refuge where they could and the revenues which the monks had previously given out to the poor and used to nurse the sick were taken for the use of the King and his nobles. The possession and revenues from this pre-bend he gave to Trinity College, Cambridge which he had just founded.

In this part of the world they clung to their old religion and this resulted in a number of uprisings. The first was 'The Pilgrimage of Grace' in 1536 and a great many people, noble and commoner alike, took part in it. It was a complete failure and many including the late Abbots of Fountains and Jervaulx were executed. At his examination the Abbot of Fountains said that Middleton and Staveley (at this time the Staveleys owned the Manor of Swinton) came to him and asked him for 40 pence. He gave them one aungell-noble and bade them change it. They said it was cracked so he gave them another and Staveley took both. The abbot was angry and Middleton told him not to pay any attention to Staveley as he was mad and he would pay back the abbot himself. About a fortnight later Middleton and Staveley came with many others and asked himself and the abbot of Jervaulx, on the pain of death, to come with them to Middleham moor. They said it was not right for religious men to go about such business and asked to be left alone. A Mr Beckwith, who was present, intervened on the abbot's behalf and they left taking the servants only. However this cannot have been a good enough defence as he was later executed.

Having got his divorce and plenty of money from the churches, Henry VIII did not proceed much further with the Reformation during the rest of his reign. But during the short reign of his son Edward VI things moved much faster; services were changed and all ornaments were ordered to be removed from the churches. It was probably at this time that our beautiful church cross was defaced, and the stone altar, the screens and lattices which separated the choir and side-chapels from the nave were removed or destroyed. Queen Mary who succeeded Edward was a Catholic and, determined to make England a Catholic country again, was ruthless in her persecution of the Protestants, putting many to death. However when Elizabeth I came to the throne the Reformation once again went ahead and many cruel laws were passed to get rid of the Catholic religion. It was death to harbour a Catholic priest, to confess to one, or even to attend a Catholic service. Anyone who did not attend their parish church to hear the new service of common prayer every Sunday was fined. In 1569 many were so dissatisfied with Elizabeth's way of dealing with religious matters that they were prepared to rise in open rebellion against her, and the Earls of Northumberland and Westmorland led an army south from Durham restoring the old services in churches as they went. When they got to Wetherby they decided they had not got as much support as they needed and decided to retreat northwards. A large Royal army pursued them and the rebels eventually lost heart and disbanded. Some escaped, others were caught and put to death, others had their possessions taken away. Although Christopher Danby did not actually join the rebel army his sympathies were certainly with it, and his son-in-law Sir John Neville was convicted of high treason for the part he took in it.

Sir Thomas Danby succeeded his father in 1571; he was married to an aunt of the Earl of Westmorland who led the rebellion. He was High Sheriff of Yorkshire in 1576 and in 1583 was a Justice of the Peace for the North Riding, of whom there were then only twenty-one. In 1565 he joined with his father in buying the manors of Healey and Ellington from Henry, Lord Scrope of Bolton and in 1586 he bought Pott from Mr William Singleton of Fountains. He built Farnley Hall at Otley in 1586. He was a person of some importance, numbering Lord Burleigh amongst his friends and his advice was sought in affairs of state. His son Thomas married Elizabeth Wentworth, an aunt of the future Earl of Strafford.

Thomas died during his father's lifetime and left a son, Christopher, who succeeded his grandfather in 1590. He was only nine years old and his mother was left with the management of the estates. She then met a cousin of her husband, also called Christopher Danby; he was very charming and talked her into giving him the management of the estates. She installed him at Leighton Hall and in doing this made the greatest mistake of her life. He was a rogue determined to make as much money he could for himself out of the estates. He dismissed the old faithful servants such as the Smorthwaites who lived at High Healey Cote and installed his own confederates. He managed to persuade Elizabeth Danby and her son to stay away with friends, during which time he lived an evil and riotous-life, selling off bits of the estate at ridiculously low prices and letting the rest fall into ruin. He tricked his mistress into borrowing money for his own use which was to cause her great trouble in the future. This state of affairs continued until young Christopher Danby came of age in 1606.[1]

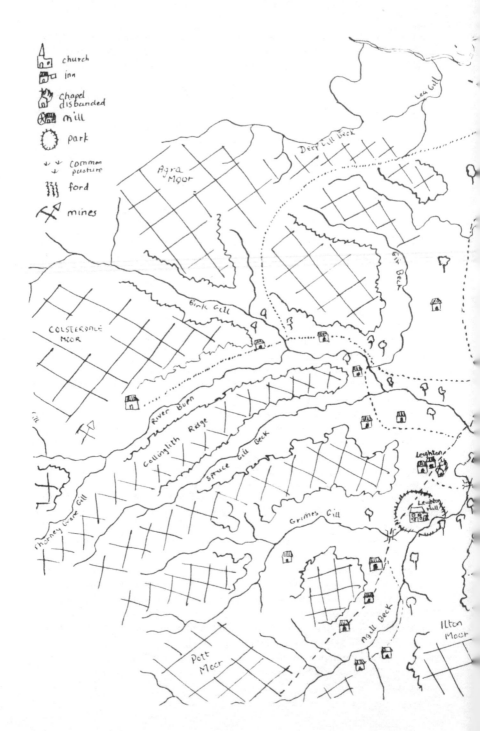

church
inn
chapel disbanded
mill
park
common pasture
ford
mines

Agra Moor

Deer Gill Beck

Lea Gill

Birk Gill

Gill Beck

COLSTERDALE MOOR

River Burn

Collinglith Ridge

Spruce Gill Beck

Thorney Grane Gill

Grimes Gill

Leighton

Leighton Hall

Agill Beck

Pott Moor

Ilton Moor

Outline map of the district during the sixteenth century

63

As timber and thatch buildings began to suffer decay farmers, being slightly more prosperous, began to replace them with stone buildings. These consisted of a large living-room and a parlour which was the master and mistress's bedroom. They now had fireplaces and chimneys. The rest of the family and the servants slept on the top floor which just consisted of lofts. Farm labourers slept in the farm buildings. There is an old barn in Fearby which dates back to this century. The North Yorkshire and Cleveland Vernacular Buildings Study Group recently did a study of this and the following are some of their conclusions and two plans they made:

The barn is of three bays divided by two ruck trusses. The north truss has a full tiebeam halved across it, from which an upper floor is built over the north end; the ground-floor room has been a kitchen with a fireplace now blocked and the remains of a former large oven. The western blocked window seems to imply an upper floor throughout with one central window.

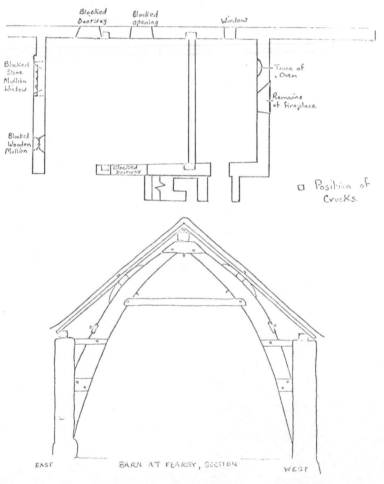

Plans by the North Yorkshire and Cleveland Vernacular Buildings Study Group of the barn at Fearby

The crucks in the barn at Fearby

A visitor to Masham in 1540 talks of a wooden bridge over the Yore and we have the following order made at Quarter Sessions at Thirsk:

It is ordered by the court that the sume of ffower hundred pounds bee estreated throughout the whole Northridd for the repaire of Massome bridge and pyd unto Thomas Thwaites of High Burton gent Thomas Smith of Massome Thomas Beckwith of Lamb Hill Symond Pickersgill of Lowe Burton and John Marshale of Massome Edward Beckwith of Nutwitz Coate and Chrystopher Croft of Massome who are appoynted Surveyors for the same to see the mony carefully disburst for the repaire thereof And that they make their accounts unto this And that Sr. Chr. Wyvill Bart and Sr. William Dalton Bt. is desired to see the money disburst accordingly.

Some of the more important families in the village at this time were the Brown family in Ilton and Ellingstring, Smorthwaites in Healey, Pickersgills in Fearby, Beckwiths at Nutwith Cote and Pott.[2] Sir Christopher Metcalfe also owned some land in Healey, and he was responsible for introducing crayfish into the Yore.

10 1600

In 1606 when he came of age young Christopher Danby returned to his estates, and from then on was to find himself in almost constant difficulties due mostly to the plotting of his steward, Christopher Danby. He had not been in Mashamshire long before he made his presence felt by taking forcible possession of Arnagill with a dozen of his friends and evicting the owner Abram Smith (this was probably one of the bits of land sold by Christopher Danby, the steward, when he had charge of the estate); he was fined by a Special Inquisition at Patrick Brompton but kept possession of Arnagill. The evil steward unjustly arranged for accusations of harbouring Catholics to be brought against Elizabeth Danby and her son in order to get them out of the way again. Young Christopher Danby fled to London and persuaded Lord Monteagle, whose father had been one of the judges at the trial of Mary Queen of Scots, to defend him.

In 1605 it was to Lord Monteagle that one of the conspirators in the Gunpowder plot wrote, warning him not to attend Parliament on November 5. It was thanks to his investigation that the plot was discovered. Since then he had been a man of great consequence and he seems to have been able to quash the accusation against Christopher Danby.

The capture of Guy Fawkes

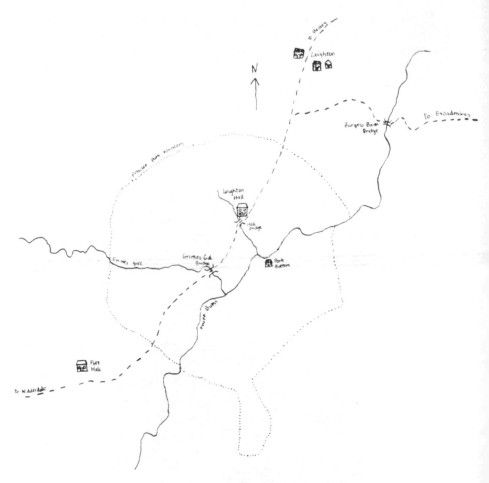

Sketch map of the site of Leighton Hall

While he was in London Christopher Danby met Lord Monteagle's sister Frances, and decided that by marrying her he would advance himself in the world. They were married in July 1607 but Lord Monteagle was not pleased with the match as he had discovered the neglected state of Christopher Danby's estates. He refused to pay the marriage portion until one-third of the family estates had been settled on his sister. The evil steward Danby saw that this would upset all his plans and he hurried to London to make trouble between the husband and his new wife. He was only too successful and within a month of the marriage Frances returned to her brother's house. However she was later persuaded to return to her husband, the dismissal of the steward probably being one of her conditions. It was now that the young Christopher Danby decided to rebuild Leighton Hall which had been left in a disgraceful state by the steward. The new steward, Miles Danby, kept exact records and from these we can see that the renovations were quite extensive:

First stage—preparation

August	2 men scoured the spring heads in the Ox		
	Close 6 days at 8d	8s	0d
August—October	2 wrights take down the walls 7 days at 10d	11s	8d
	The mason 53 days at 4d	17s	8d
	2 men in the lime pits 30 days at 6d	£1 10s	0d
	1 man in the slate pit 22 days at 6d	11s	0d
	4 loads of slate	8s	6d

Second stage—roofing and glassing

November	2 wrights line the spars and slate the house	18s	2d
	Smith's bill	9s	2d
	Glassiner: 110 ft of new glass	£2 15s	0d
	26 ft of old glass resetting	6s	8d
December	2 wrights 23 days at 4d	15s	4d
	1 mason 21 days at 4d	7s	0d
	1 mason 12 days at 4d	4s	0d
	Glassiner: 18 ft new glass	14s	0d
	10 ft old glass	2s	6d
	Mending high leads and plastering windows	2s	0d

Third stage—furnishing and interior

January–March	2 joiners 32 days at 6d	£1 12s	0d
	Workmen	7s	10d
	Smith of Leeds: doorbands, crooks and locks	£1 3s	2d
	Workmen who laid stones for a 'suer' [probably		
	a channel for pure water]	1s	0d
February	Miles Danby went to Thirsk, Ripon and Masham		
	for bed-posts and curtains	1s	11d
	Upholsterer's bills	£2 14s	4d
April	Mrs Smorthwaite bought utensils at Richmond	£2 0s	0d
	Rich. Smorthwaite brought bedding from		
	Farnley Hall	10s	0d

Fourth stage—gardening

April	2 wrights move the park pale 70 days at 6d	£3 10s	0d
	Work in the garden: (including 9 days		
	by head gardener at 1s)	£2 1s	3d
April 14	The first visitors (Christopher Danby of		
	Masham, another kinsman, brought his family		
	to Leighton)	£1 18s	4d
May–July	Work in the garden (including 12 days by head		
	gardener at 1s)		
September	3 plumbers for fastening the leads	£2 4s	0d
	5 lbs of iron for gargoyles	1s	8d
	2 wrights made hall chimney	6s	0d
December 14th	Lord Latimer at Leighton		
		£29 16s	4d

Riding the stang (*Costume of Yorkshire, 1814*)

The young Christopher Danby's mother bought Pott Grange off her son and lived there. The dismissed steward Danby continued to make trouble and spread the rumour that Christopher Danby was ill-using his wife and it was only by the vigilance of his new steward that the servants were withheld from 'stanging' him. To ride the stang two men would parade the street with a pole on their shoulders, carrying an image of the offending husband: the crowd followed shouting

Tam-a-ran, tam-a-ran, tan, tan,
It's not for my part or their part that I ride the stang,
But it's for .... his wife he did bang.

However the steward Danby continued to harass them with accusations of harbouring Catholic priests, taking possession of a part of the estate and forcing them to take him to court to get him out and then reletting to his friends, whom he had tricked Elizabeth Danby into borrowing money from, and then also sued young Christopher Danby for debt, who consequently finished his life shut up in Leighton Hall; persecuted by his enemies, neglected by his friends and weakened by continual sickness, he lacked the spirit to attempt anything. His mother was the only one who stood by him and she survived him living on at Pott Hall doing her utmost to save the estate and continuing to take a keen interest in national affairs. She died at Thorpe Perrow in 1629.[1]

The young Christopher Danby's eldest son Thomas succeeded him but as he was a minor of only fourteen years of age he became a ward of the Court of Wards and Liveries. Sir Christopher Wandesford of Kirklington was persuaded by Sir Thomas Wentworth, nephew of Elizabeth Danby, and later Lord Strafford, to buy his wardship and brought him up with his own children. He later married Catherine Wandesford, one of Sir Christopher's daughters, and they lived on at Kirklington for a while as they were considered too young to set up house on their own (she was only fifteen).

Thomas Danby as a child, by J. Carleton 1635 (Swinton collection)

Thomas Wentworth, 1st Earl of Strafford—painting studio of Vandyck
1636 (National Portrait Gallery)

In 1633 Sir Christopher Wandesford was appointed Master of the Rolls in Ireland and took his family there. The Danbys then went to live at Farnley Hall. Thomas Danby was made Deputy Lieutenant of the West Riding by his cousin Lord Strafford who was then Lord Lieutenant, and he was appointed colonel of a regiment of soldiers.

It was at this time that Charles I quarrelled with Parliament eventually dismissing it altogether and attempting to rule the country as an absolute monarch. He appointed Sir Thomas Wentworth as his advisor making him Lord Wentworth and later Earl of Strafford. In 1634 Charles promised to help the King of Spain against the Dutch and to supply a certain number of ships. The people of England were no friends of the Spaniards and did not wish to provide ships and certainly not if Parliament had not authorised the payment of taxes for them. But Charles I sent collectors through the country to raise the taxes and, in trying to help his cousin Lord Wentworth, Thomas Danby was very active in enforcing the payment of these taxes which made both his cousin and his King very unpopular in the country.

Thomas Danby also represented the borough of Richmond in Parliament and was member during the memorable Long Parliament. This was when the Scots invaded England and the King having no money was forced to summon Parliament. It sat for 19 years. The first thing it did was to impeach Lord Wentworth (now Lord Strafford) because they said he had raised an army in Ireland which he intended to bring to England to put down Parliament. This was quite untrue as he had been sent to Ireland by Charles I to restore order, which he did quite ruthlessly. He defended himself bravely before Parliament and Thomas Danby came forward and gave evidence on his behalf at the trial and voted against his conviction. Danby was thus marked a Royalist and in 1642 was declared incapable of sitting in Parliament because of his Royalist beliefs. Parliament found Strafford guilty and sentenced him to death and the King, to his eternal shame, signed his death warrant.

Thomas Danby continued to fight for the cause of the Cavaliers and, as the Roundheads gained power, suffered for his beliefs. He was a prisoner for a time and had to pay a fine of £5600 to procure his freedom and for the restoration of his estates. His wife died at Thorpe Perrow in 1645 leaving him with fourteen children. After the Restoration, when Charles II became King, he invested Thomas Danby with the Order of the Royal Oak as a mark of, and reward for, his loyalty. He did not live long after this, dying in August 1660. He was succeeded by his son, another Thomas Danby, who had been a Captain in the Royal Army and was the first Mayor of Leeds. He died in 1667 and was succeeded by his son Thomas who died in 1671, and then by his next son Christopher who was killed by a fall from his horse on Watlass-moor whilst hunting in 1683, and thus died a minor. He was succeeded by his uncle Christopher Danby who the same year made over the estates to his son Abstrupus Danby.[2]

Abstrupus found the estates heavily mortgaged and set about putting them in order. He then bought the remaining one-third of the manor of Swinton from Mr Norton; he built a manor house at Swinton about 1695 and moved there from

The old Hall at Swinton, 1723

Thorpe Perrow. He was a Justice of the Peace and a Deputy Lieutenant for the North Riding. We have an interesting insight into how a large house was run in those days from notes which Lady Danby wrote on the work of the various servants—the following are some extracts:[3]

The office of a cook maid as I conceive, is, to take care of ye dressing of all ye meat fish flesh and foule and make to each their proper sauses belonging to them and to look to ye wett larder for ye salting of ye macklemas beef bacon, and to ye preserving of all under her care sweet and good fitt for her Masters table, to wash up and clean all her kitchen vessell and keep them in their places, yt none of their number be lost, she is to keep her kitchen, larders, scullery, stillhouse, small beare Seller, ye little hall where ye Servants dine and pantery clean, and when we kill a Swine and beefe she is to take care to ye washing ye belly to ye tups feet and poddings, and when ye belly is to be washt ye daire maid is to help her do it and to make ye poddings, and to help her Scouer ye pewter, and when we wash ye Cook maid must wash as long as she can.

The housekeeper's office is to looke yt all ye servants performe there places, yt all things and places be kept clean and in order yt nothing be lost or out of its place to help and see diner served up hamsomly, to make all fine podings, made dishes, coups and all pretty curiosity for yt are gentle and hamson to set out a table, to raise past, preserve, make wines cordeals, to have skill in surgury and to know and how to help and tend in sickness, to do all yt is needfull in a country place where we have no help nere us.

The office of the chamber maid is to know how to dress me and my heads to wash and starch all ye mussling and fine linning all yt belongs to her Master and me and my Son, and to make and mend all yt belongs to us, to keep my Chamber neat and to help ye house maid to Clean all ye Chambers and rooms above Stairs.

The office of a butler is in ye first place to ley ye cloth and Sidebord neat and hamsome for ye credite of ye house and take care of all ye linning belongs to ye table, to deliver out ye number is to be washt and to look to take in ye Same again when tis clean or when any of it is to be mended to take notice what is given out yt he may see to ye takeing ye Same in again. He is to take charge of ye plate, to keep it neat and clean and to take care to ye washing ye glasses, and to ye cleaning ye knives and forks and ye candlesticks, yt belong to ye dineing roome yt is in his care, he is to take ye charge of ye Sellers, to see ye drink after tis brought in and has done working be well Stopt yt it may drink fresh to ye last, and when ye vessils want keeping to send for ye Cooper, and to See yt he hoops them tite and well yt they leak not to wast ye drink, he is to bottle all ye March and October drink and to wash ye bottles and in generall to keep ye Sellers neat and Clean and to do all thinks yt belongs to ye office of a Butler, tho it may be omitted here in Setting down, he is to understand how to comb, curle, tye, powder and ole his Masters wiggs, and to shave them, to dress and waite on them in there Chambers, to go abroad with him when tis required, and to write for him what he has occation for when at home, he is to clean their shooes and boots and to liquor them when they need it. He is likewise to keep ye graniry and to deliver out ye malt for Brueing and to take an account of what Malt he takes into ye Granary, yt ye going out and comeing in may exactly answer on ye other, and ye same care is to be taken of what quantity of wheat he receives into ye grain and how much he delivers out to be ground at ye mill for bread for ye

Sir Abstrupus Danby—style of Garret (Swinton collection)

house use and likewise to take an account of what corne and provender comes into ye granery yt belongs to ye horses. and to mesure it out to ye Coachman and husbandman ye allowance yt his Master Shall order for every horse. and neither give more nor less. yt what he receives in and what he delivers out of all things in ye grainry and in his Charge may agree together yt he may give a faithfull and true account to his master when he Shall require it.

The office of a dairy maid is to take care of ye milking of ye cows and to make ye butter and Cheese and curds what elce belongs to ye house. and for Servants and to clean and scald all her boulds and all things belonging to her dairie. and to feed and fat all ye poultrey and to keep them clean or they will not thrive. and when they are to be used. to pull them and make them fitt for ye Spit and to keep ye fethers dry yt they be not Spoyl'd. and likewise to feed and fat ye Swine for pork and bacon. to boult all ye flower to make Brown bread to keep ye meal house and brue house clean to clean ye men Servants lodgings once a week and all yt row of buildings to help ye cook maide wash ye bellys of her beefes and make black podings for Servants and to help Scoure ye pewter brass and all other things then. and to help to was ye course and other linning.

ye men must make their owne beds all ye week themselves

The office of the house and wash maids is to help to clean all ye house in generall above Staires and ye parlor and great hall below Staires. to help to wash and to get up all ye linning from ye beginning to ye end. to mend all ye Course linning and table cloths. to wash ye wolling as potticots wascots stockings curtings &c to help ye daire maid to milk all ye Sommer when ye milk at ye hight yt She cannot carry it her Self but when it grows less yt She can. She must do it by her Self. she must help ye Cook maid to scoure ye pewter. and what else there is occation for yt at present comes not to my mind.

There are also four pages of directions on what the cook maid has to do every minute of the day both winter and summer!

The Puritans became more powerful in the church at this time and in 1649 the Reverend Benjamin Browne the rightful vicar of Masham was turned out of his parish and replaced by a succession of Puritan vicars until the Restoration when Mr Browne was restored to his living. Matthew Beckwith. a son of Roger Beckwith of Aldborough Hall. was one of Cromwell's captains and a Justice of the Peace for the North Riding. and as such was very active in putting laws into force not only against the Roman Catholics but such as presumed to differ from him in matters of religion. What ornaments that had been left in the church during the Reformation were removed during the supremacy of the Puritans, and it is most probable that it was at this time that the altar-rails. tresselated pavement and the stained-glass windows were broken down and removed and the church was left in a great state of neglect. After the Restoration work went ahead to restore the church and the following are some items from the church warden's accounts:

1695	Paid the workmen for poyntinge the spire	£13 0s 0d
	Paid for a load of malt and bruinge it and carryin it to church	18s 3d
1696	Paid Joseph Pickersgill for making 3 new windows	£1 14s 6d
	Paid to John Robinson for Ironworke for churchwardenes and bells	£1 15s 0d

Lady Danby—style of Garret (Swinton collection)

Old part of Aldburgh Hall

| 1699 | Paid to Joseph Pickersgill, glazier for makinge 1 new window and mendinge several other windowes | £1 2s 10d |
| 1702 | Paid to Joseph Pickersgill for makinge 2 new windowes | £1 12s 6d |

It was at this time that we have the first mention of the Four and Twenty of Masham when Sir Roger Beckwith, a Puritan, objected to the money the churchwardens were spending on improving the church. They claimed that they only had to present their accounts to the Four and Twenty and when they were approved that was all right. They had then seemingly been in existence for some time and, prior to 1662 when the parish had been divided into townships, they had been responsible for all the poor in the parish. Apart from approving the churchwarden's accounts they were also responsible for appointing three of the four churchwardens, the fabric of the church, erection of pews, appointment of sexton and the right to appoint new members to fill any vacancies in their number.[4]

At the end of the last century and the beginning of this the Peculier Court of Masham, which since the Reformation had been in the control of Trinity College, had to deal with a great number of parishioners, many of whom objected to the new religion, and who were brought before it for many offences including the following:

not coming to church enough,
keeping their hats on at communion time,
not coming to church on Sundays and holidays,
for bidding the churchwardens to do their worst on being asked to go to church,
not receiving communion three times a year,
refusing to learn the church catechism,
not bringing their children to be baptised.

getting married without banns or licence,
not getting married in their own parish church,
being married by a Roman Catholic priest,
for husband and wife living apart,
schoolmasters teaching without a licence,
for drunkenness,
for swearing,
for brawling and scolding,
for being common scolds,
for telling fortunes and using unlawful enchantments,
for harbouring Roman Catholic priests,
for allowing mass to be said in their houses,
the churchwardens for not imposing a fine of 12d every time a person was absent from church,
the clergyman for not reading 'The Book of Sports' during the service as required by the King's Proclamation,
for being suspected of being a Roman Catholic,
for carrying a dead man's skull out of the churchyard and laying it under the head of a person to charm him to sleep![5]

Although there were no proper schools there were a number of schoolmasters who had to be licenced and, for a fee, would teach a number of children in their homes. We find the following being brought to the Peculier Court for Teaching without a licence:

Henry Pickard, Masham
Simon Lambert, Ilton
John Sanderson, Healey
Mark Smith, Fearby
? Page, Healey
Thomas Slaiter, Ellingstring.

The seal of the Peculier of Masham

Old chimney and window in College House which is said to have been the Court House belonging to Trinity College

Many of our oldest stone houses date from this century. The Mill House in Masham is thought to have been built then as it is part of the old Mill itself. Lobley Hall which is now a ruin has the date 1698 on its lintel, and Ghyll Head farmhouse is dated 1689. Lobley Hall as its name suggests was most probably once a manor house for the manor of Ilton ('Hall' was always a word used for a large or manor house). The five fields lying between it and Hilltop farm are named 'park' which indicates that there was once a park attached to it.

We find the Old Hall in Masham (now Park House, see opposite page) mentioned in some deeds; it was bought by Mrs Danby in 1604 and sold again by her in 1624 to Simon Pickersgill. Nutwith Cote, which had been in the hands of the Beckwiths since it was owned by Fountains Abbey, was taken by Marmaduke Smorthwaite in 1633; in 1662 Catherine Smorthwaite married Simon Bartlett.

80

Mill House

Park House

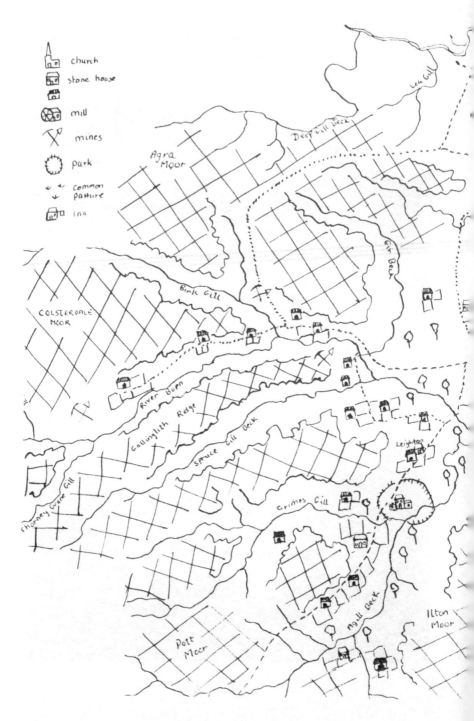

church
stone house

mill
mines
park
common pasture
Inn

Agra Moor
Deep Gill Beck
Lea Gill
Elk Beck
Birk Gill
COLSTERDALE MOOR
River Burn
Collinglith Ridge
Spruce Gill Beck
Thorney Grane Gill
Grimes Gill
Leighton
Pott Moor
Agill Beck
Ilton Moor

82

Outline map of the district during the seventeenth century

The following are some of the rents paid during the seventeenth century:[6]

Hallgarth	£40
High Mains	£40
Masham and Swinton Mills	£50
Healey Mill	£12
Low Mains	£15
Low Ashhead	£12 10s
Moorheads and Leighton	£107 12s

The rents taken from the villages were:

Masham	£119 17s 4d
Healey	£92 14s 2d
Fearby	£31 19s 4d
Swinton	£67

The following were some of the offences for which you would be brought before the Manor Court in 1663:

not keeping up fences,
not ringing swine,
taking alders from between Swinton and Healey Mills,
taking timber from High Ox Close,
breaking hedges,
assault for which the scale of fines seems to be:

assault	1s 8d
affray	3s 4d
drawing blood	6s 8d–10s

In 1633 the tolls at Masham market were:

every bull, cow, ox or heifer	1d
every horse, mare or gelding	1d
every colt	1d
every 5 sheep	1d
every 5 lambs	1d
every boar	2d
every hogg, sow or other pig	2d

These were to be paid between the buyer and seller equally:

every bushel of grain	half a pint
every horseload of grain sold and carried out of these markets	½d

11 1700

There seems to have been some disharmony between Abstrupus Danby Senior and Abstrupus Danby Junior as can be seen from the following letters from the young Abstrupus Danby to Robert Arthington of Farnley Hall:[1]

Swinton, March 31st 1703

My Kind ffreind,

Tho' I once thought I Should never be guilty of a Crime so detestable as in-gratitude, yet I now find it somewhat difficult to acquitt my selfe, at least from the imputation of it, in having neglected to write to a person I so justly Esteem as your selfe. I cannot forget the engagements I have to ffarnley, not only those I received on it's own account by the natural pleasantness which reign's there, but also those I derived from yr. selfe and good ffamily by the kind treatment and civility y.o obliged me withall when I was there. But I have not yet done thanking you (for w)hat me (. . . . .) behind, (a)nd that is yr. good wishes yo. express for me in my marriage, and the kind advice yo. give my ffather upon yt. subject which so highly relates to my quiet and satisfaction as long as I live. I have sent along with Lance a mare I lately bought for which I gave a great price and which I highly value. I intend her (provided my ffather will bestow her on me) for my own riding, but pray don't show him her when he comes down for I suppose he intends to come yr. way whenever he returns, for I wd. first tell him of her, after some time, my selfe. She is not till May four years old 'till which time I also pray yo. to keep her in the house else there will be no grass for her. I desire you to take all immaginable care of her, and I mean to let her run the following summer and winter together with part of the summer after at which time shee'l come six and then shee'l be a topper for I ha(ve g)reat hopes on her and value her extremely therefore once more I intreat yo. to take care of her which will great add to the obligacens of yr.

most Affectionate and truly real
freind in every sense

Abstrupus Danby

My kind and Dear Freind Robert,

I had wrote to you before this, but that I thought it more proper to defer writing, 'till you had confer'd with my Knight; to the end that I might receive an Account of his Royall Will and pleasure, from your Selfe. This I confess I shall be glad to Hear, when you are dispos'd and at leisure, but to deal truly with you, I can of myself almost prognosticate the Result of your Conversation, by the little Discourse I had with him here; which does still add to my beliefe that he will not do what in Fatherly kindness with great Ease he Might, as well as with Honour to himselfe and security to his ffortunes. But I am now pretty well satisfied, that tho' I should (in Christian Charity) put the most favourable Construction upon his designs, which he so Violently and Unthinkingly pursues; yet upon due Reflection I am fully Convinc'd they will (if resolutely persisted in) most Certainly Terminate in the Utter ruin of that Idol he so much Worships (his Estate) as well as in the Destruction of his Son. I have at last with much ado, prevail'd on him to let me go up to Town next Winter; and likewise that my Mother shall go up with me. I shall be very glad if he will but stand to his word, which he never cou'd yet do in anything of Moment, where my Wishes and True Interest were Concern'd. Upon prefering to him my petition About going to Lond. next winter, his honre. was pleas'd to be a little disorder'd with passion, and very wittily ask'd me whether I wou'd have him Mortgage a peice of Land for that purpose, for that he did not Otherwise know how to Supply me with Money. I likewise requested him to Advance my Allowance Assuring him at the same time that 'twas Impossible to live at Lond. (or indeed anywhere else) Credibly upon what he at present permitted me to Enjoy. But still with the same prudence and ingenuity, as well as ffatherly kindness, he did with a few widemouth'd Oaths tenderly Assure me, that he cou'd by no means do it, since that after Law-Suits, Taxes, and Other Incumbrances were satisfied, he had then no more than £400 a year let. So finding him in such a pretty, reasonable, Obliging Humour, I left off my Sollicitations in relation to his Adding to my Allowance. After all, I intreat you but to Judge, between God and your own Conscience, whether he be not a most kind and Excellent ffather; who out of an Estate of more than £2,200 a year when 'tis Clear, and whereof notwithstanding he at present enjoys at least £1,000 if not £1,200 to himselfe. And yet this good ffather is not Able (or rather can't find in his heart) to allow his only, or at least his Eldest Son, (and I hope a person of no ill Character) £200 a year; which I presume is an allowance no man in his right witts can think extravagant for such an Estate. I could say much more, but 'tis in vain; and therefore I shall Submit all to Gods Disposal, and endeavour as far as I am Able like a Man and a Christian to await his time who doubtless knows what's best for us, and will at last release every one who repose their trust in him. I am (and do ever desire to remain) without fraud or Guile

Your obliged and most Affectionate Freind

Abstrupus Danby

The gates at Swinton

However in 1727 Sir Abstrupus Danby died and was succeeded by his son. He does not seem to have done much by which to be remembered and was in turn succeeded by his son William in 1750, a person of great intelligence and good taste, with active business habits of which he made full use in the improvement of his estates and the way of life of the people who lived in it. He reclaimed and brought into profitable cultivation much of the moorlands. He also considerably improved his house at Swinton, making quite a number of alterations in 1767. He built the stables in 1752–53 and the gates in 1754. In the 1760s he laid out a chain of lakes in the park but these were considerably altered by his son.

The stables at Swinton

Swinton Park by R. Sykes 1790

Rape threshing (*Costume of Yorkshire, 1814*)

These improvements attracted considerable attention at the time, and in 1768 he received a visit from Arthur Young, the eminent agricultural author of that period; the following are some extracts from the notes written by Mr Young about the visit. Firstly about the method of agriculture:

Their courses of husbandry are 1st fallow—2nd wheat—3rd beans.

Another course is 1st fallow—2nd wheat—3rd turnips.

For wheat they plough four or five times——sow from nine to eleven pecks about Michaelmas and reckon to average two and a half quarters.

For barley they plough three times, sow from ten to twelve pecks in April and gain at a medium the same quantity as of wheat.

For oats they give but one stirring, sow four and a half bushels in March, and reckon the mean crop at three quarters. . . .

It is known amongst the farmers that such a practice as hoeing exists, and some of them begin to talk of it but very few have practised it.

The average value per acre is £2 10s.

They plough once or twice for rape, sow it at the end of July, never feed it—sow wheat after it—know nothing of clover.

Pay very little attention to raising large quantities of manure—their principal dependence is upon lime, of which they lay from one to two and a half chaldrons per acre.

Good grass lets from 20s to 25s per acre.

The summer joist of a cow from 20s to 25s.

The annual expense of a horse (including shoeing) they reckon at £7.

Woman spinning (*Costume of Yorkshire, 1814*)

Poor-rates twopence to fivepence in the pound—at Masham tenpence.

The employment, spinning of worsted: a women earns, if industrious, sixpence or eightpence a day.

All drink tea.

Price of labour, etc. in harvest 26s or 28s and board and lodging.

In hay-time a mower 30s a month and board and lodging—in winter sixpence a day and board and lodging.

Mowing grass two shillings per acre.

First man's wages £10 to £13——next ditto £7. Boy of ten or twelve years £3—dairymaids, £5 other maids £3 10s to £4 4s. Women per day in harvest tenpence or one shilling—in haytime sevenpence to eightpence—in winter sixpence.

Price of provisions, cheese 2d butter 8d the 22 ounces—beef 3d mutton 3d veal 3d pork 3½d—milk one halfpenny the one and a half pint—potatoes 3½d the peck—turnips 3d ditto—candles 6½d and 1b soap 7d the lb. Labourer's house-rent 15s to 40s. Firing 15s.

He also tells of a tenant, Mr Lightfoot, who grows cabbages and finds them very profitable. He then goes on to write about the colliery:

Mr. Danby has a colliery upon the edge of his moors which employs many hands. The cottages of the colliers are scattered about at no great distance. Each had at first a small garden, which from the great foresight and refined politics (for I can give the conduct no other name) of their landlord grew into little farms. Great praise is here given to Mr Danby for his judgement and kindness towards the miners, and after their own farms are in good cultivation, he encloses part of the moor for their use, which after some years they pay a trifling rent.

Lowkers (*Costume of Yorkshire, 1814*)

He writes of one particular collier, James Croft:

He started with one acre pared and burnt the heather limed and ploughed it. He continued liming, sowing a variety of crops for a number of years until he had turned it into good grassland. He then took in another eight acres, three of these were very stoney and it took him two months to clear one of these, breaking up the big stones and carting them away. He gradually brought these eight acres into cultivation and then took over another eight acres. He did all this at the same time as working down the mine which with his meals took up twelve hours of the day. He never had more than four hours sleep and on moonlight nights less than that. He spread a great deal of lime on his land which he had to bring from six miles away and he also ploughed his land a great many times each winter—to help him with this he had one old horse. His ambition was to see more moorland brought back to be good grassland.

Mr Young says that his grassland was as good as that of any he came across during his tour of the cultivated counties. He also writes of the lovely walk through Hackfall which was then landscaped with seats, grottos and waterfalls.

This was a very active time in the collieries in Colsterdale and there are a great many records remaining.[2] The following are some entries from the banksman's books:

1692

May 9	Paid to Geo Nawthorp for ten dozen of candles	£1	5s 0d
April 26	To Mr Wm Borkwith for iron and powder	£1	1s 2½d
	To Geo. Holdsworth for walling and slating ye Smithy		4s 0d
	To Henry Loftus for bring a load of iron to the pits		5d

91

Traces of a slag heap in Colsterdale

	To John Tollow for pulling and coaring 5		
	thrave of ling to the Smithy	2s	6d
	For thatching the Smithy	1s	2d
May 24	Paid to Rich. Ascough and Thos. Allan for		
	driving 20 yds in a New Groove called		
	Allans Groove by a bargain	£2 3s	0d
	Paid to Wm Borkwith for iron & Stool &		
	ten pound of powder	£1 13s	0½d
1714	Paid for a lantern for ye miners to go to		
	work with at night	1s	10d

We also have a schedule of all the worktools belonging to Abstrupus Danby in 1734:

20 gavlacks, 48 coal picks, 21 iron mells, 28 iron wedges, 8 hacks, 11 new chains for ye lads to draw corves with, 1 nail-tool and several pieces of iron, 5 wimbles, a blasting gavlack, 3 pair of tongs, 1 fireporr shovel, 3 hammers.

We also have notes on the pits and groves worked from 1690 to 1801 and a map showing their positions.[3] Nowadays, apart from a few slag tips, there are very few traces left. Some of the old entrances, ruined buildings and tracks can still be found if you search among the heather and bracken. Lead was mined in Bell Gill pit between 1700 and 1723, and the colliery was one of the first to use gunpowder for blasting.

In 1753 an agreement was made between the miners and William Danby that they should use only Masham and Healey water-mills for grinding their corn. The name of 29 colliers were on the agreement, most of them making their mark as they could not write their names.

Notes on coal mines 1826

1690 Thorney Grain High Pit. Little grove. Middle pit. Nab end Pit and Brownbeck

1691 Sander Pit. Bell Gill pit. coals sold at 5d per corf

1692 Bell Gill and Middle pits principally wrought

1693 Sander Pit and Rantry Grove

1697 New Grove. Stable Pit and Smithy Grove

1699 New Grove. High Grove. and Smithy Grove

1701 Some of the above pits and Brownbeck

1704 Loftus Grove and in 1705 Engine pit

1708 Bell Gill pit. Smithy and Dawson's Groves

1709 New pit. Wabron pit. Ned Grove. Butt Pit. Bell Gill pit and Nab end pit

1711 Bog Pit and Darby Grove—from 2000–2800 corves got every month in Darby Grove. the workmen was compelled to get 14 corves each day at $1\frac{3}{4}$–2d a corf

1713 Darby Grove. engine and Bog pits

1715 April. Mr Robinson (Banksman) accounts finished. who was succeeded by Richard Ascough

1718 Darby Grove. Allan Grove and Walker Grove—in December this year Richard Ascough was turned out as Banksman and succeeded by William Alderson. who continued until the year 1720. and was then succeeded by Thomas Theakston

1724 Brownbeck and Gollinglythe was wrought
     1725 Crooked Oak Grove was wrought also in 1726

1727 Middle Ruckle Grove. Francis Glue then banksman

1730 New level and Paddock Grove

1732 Dawson. Allan and Loftus Grove

1734 Sand and Crabtree Grove

1737 Allan and Loftus Grove

1741 Speedwell pit and Darby Grove—note. Speedwell pit was sunk in 1736—the boring cost £42 4s 4d they bored 25 fathoms besides the bandstone—the sinking cost exclusive of boring—£22 17s 9d

1745 Darby and Dawson Groves

1749 Dawson and Crooked Oak Groves

1752 Charity. Thorney and Tuany Groves

1760 Same and Ralph's Groves

1764 Walker and Thorney Grove

1780 Rock. Ned and Bog Grove—note. there was both a fire and Line coal colliery at this time and the Drawer (attending) was allowed 4d week for each colliery

1786 Croft Grove—note. a trial made about this time at Healey pasture end an estimate made of the Expence of a water engine there estimated at about £115

1789 Croft Grove—very few coals got then

1792 Thorney Grove

1797 Brownbeck. Bog and Ned Groves—note. all the coals got then were Line Coals but the greatest part of them was got at Brownbeck

1801 The same pits wrought then as in 1797

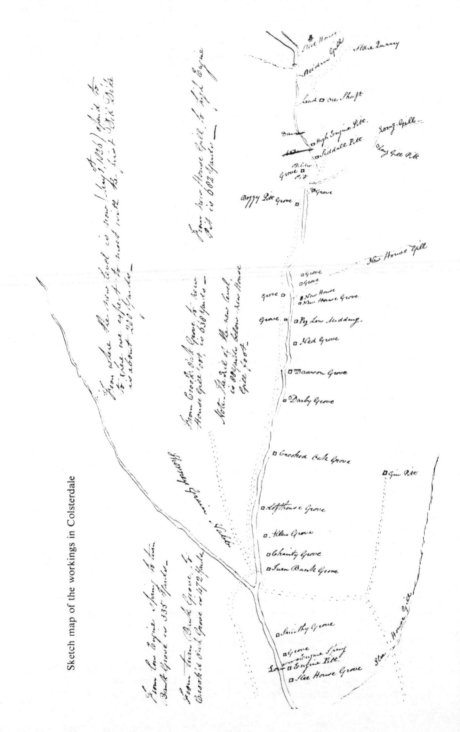

Sketch map of the workings in Colsterdale

94

As more corn was grown in the lowlands and became more easily available to the dalespeople through their local markets, fewer of them grew their own. In the more exposed parts this had always been difficult because of the climate. This meant there was less corn for the mills to grind and some were changed over to spinning cotton and worsted. One of the Healey mills (the present Swinton sawmill) became a cotton-mill. The corn-mill at Burton had fallen into decay in 1729 but in 1792 it was rebuilt as a worsted-mill. The corn-mill at Swinton was still being used and was leased by John Vitty for £6 10s a year.

Apart from Arthur Young's notes we have a good deal of material telling us what farming was like during the eighteenth century. There is a list of the tithes taken by Trinity College in 1756 which gives us an idea of the amount of money being made out of farming. We also have a survey done for Trinity College in 1791 which tells us the acreages under different forms of cultivation. Barns were built in fields with room for hay and keeping a few cows in during the winter. This saved labour in carting the hay during the summer and spreading muck in the spring. Trinity College had three tithe barns for collecting their tithes which were taken in kind.

Tithe barn at Ellingstring

95

Masham Mill by Julius Caesar Ibbetson (Swinton collection)

Healey Cotton Mill (now Swinton saw mill)

Rents paid by some of the farmers in 1728 were as follows:[4]

Stonefold	£13
Healey Cote	£30 10s
Arnagill	£14
Roundhill	£31
Pickersgill	£7 10s
Lows Mains	£45

Servants' wages:

Foreman at High Mains	£9
Carter	£6 7s 6d
Gardener	£10

Some farmer's expenses:

Shears	£3 14s 6d
Ox	£6 17s 6d
Heifer	£7 10s
New shoe for horse	4d
Killing and cutting up a pig, calf or 4 sheep	1s

The town pastures in 1745 were Marfield, Numming field, Foxholme, and High and Low Holme.

Tithes in Masham taken in 1756[5]

	£	s	d
The Tithes of Masham Town were let to Mr Robertson in 1741 and he held them several years at £47 15s 0d per year the said tythes are now let to Mr Danby at £50	50		
Jane Bullen pays more for a separate part of Masham which she occupies	7	0	0
High and Low Elington and Sutton Penns Tythes let to Chris. Jackson, Thos. Jackson, Robert Smorfit and Claron Jackson at	37	0	0
Thos. Waits of Low Elington bids more for them			
Ellingstring Tythes let to Mosas Jackson at	14	2	6
Swinton and Watermask Tythes let to Wm. Whitelock at	24	0	0
Hillton Tythes let to Mark Hutchinson, Pr. Hutchinson, Ralph Horseman, William Leasoot, Tho. Walker and Thos. Jackson at	18	0	0
Low Burton Tythes let to Henry Proctor, the corn at £7 sheep at £4	11	0	0
Wm. Wrather pays more for part of Low Burton called Thompson Farm	2	5	0
Ann Baley pays for the manor House	1	10	0
Chris. Ripley the college Tennant's agent lets the Glebe Land and 2 Parsons Closes being 17 acres to many different people these one with another are worth 10s per acre	8	11	3
Ripley lets a little close or garth joining to the manor house at	1	10	0
The said Ripley lets part of a Sheep Tythe belonging to Swinton formerly let to Wittlock at		13	0
Fearby Tythes are taken in kind by the said Ripley the College Tennants agent. In this place are kept about a thousand good sheep about 3 fleeces and ½ to yc. stone worth 18d per fleece. The Tythe of which comes to £7 10s also 500 lambs worth 3s 6d per lamb, the Tythe of which is 50 lambs worth £8 15s. The corn and Hay Tythe is worth £6 per year	22	5	0
The Tythes of Healey are taken in kind by Chris. Ripley. These tythes consist of wool and lambs only there being a modus paid for Hay and corn Tythes. In this place are kept 600 sheep the tythe of which is 60 fleeces and 15d per fleece and about 300 lambs. The tythe of which is 30 lambs at 3s 6d per lamb	9	0	0
Moorheads Tythes is also taken in kind by the said Ripley and in this place are kept 2190 Sheep the Tythe of which is 219 fleeces worth 14d per fleece and 80 tythe lambs at 3s 4d per lamb	26	0	0
	£235	6	9

Acreages under different forms of cultivation

Masham
Arable land—209 acres (wheat 90, barley 21, oats 35, beans 7, fallow 24, turnips 29)
Meadow and pasture land—1161 acres
350 sheep and 280 lambs

Swinton
Arable land—143 acres (wheat 32, barley 8, oats 51, pease 5, fallow 15, turnips 30)
Meadow land—332 acres
Pasture land—700 acres
200 sheep and 100 lambs

Ilton
Arable land—41 acres (wheat 14, barley 7, oats 9, fallow 6, turnips 4)
Meadow land—167 acres
Pasture land—238 acres
964 acres at Moorheads were claimed to be tithe free as they were Abbey land
16 large sheep and 6 lambs, 120 small sheep and 5 lambs

Ellington
Arable land—244 acres (wheat 78, barley 17, oats 65, pease 5, fallow 43, turnips 34)
Meadow and pasture land—1005 acres
550 sheep and 350 lambs, 14 small sheep and 13 lambs

Ellingstring
Arable land—67 acres (wheat 12, oats 40, fallow 6, turnips 8)
Meadow land—136 acres
Pasture land—76 acres
32 sheep and 15 lambs

Fearby—Broadmire
Arable land—113 acres (wheat 16, oats 28, rape 27, fallow 10, turnips 30)
Grassland—78 acres
Arable in remainder of Fearby—81 (wheat 22, oats 30, barley 2, fallow 18, turnips 7)

Grassland—519 acres
60 sheep and 50 lambs

Healey—Sutton Pens
Arable land—95 (42 wheat, oats 21, beans 4, pease 5, fallow 17, turnips 4)
Meadow land—56 acres
Pasture land—157 acres
100 sheep and 60 lambs
The rest of Healey seems to have been tithe free for one reason or another.

Burton upon Ure
Low Burton Farm
Arable land—95 acres (wheat 24, oats 5, beans 22, pease 16, fallow 13, turnips 14)
Meadow land—45 acres
Pasture land—183 acres
High Burton was free from paying tithes as it paid a modus instead.
Aldburgh and Nutwith Cote were also tithe free as they had belonged to Fountains Abbey.

Commons
1927 sheep and 582 lambs, 4506 small sheep and 1058 lambs

Peat cart (*Costume of Yorkshire, 1814*)

William Danby made many agreements with the inhabitants of the district giving them leave to pull heather, cut peat and collect flagstones from Steel House Gill. Heather was used for lighting fires, making besoms (brooms) and for thatching houses. For thatching it was gathered between January and April, pulled up by the roots. Five handfuls were fastened into loggins of which 24 made a theave. Gathering 5 theaves was a day's work, paying 9d a theave. The theaves were brought down from the moor by a horse and sledge and fixed to the roof with roots

Woman making oatcakes (*Costume of Yorkshire, 1814*)

100

upwards. Peat was cut for fuel from about 1200 and was used by everyone until coal became easier to get. Rushes were gathered for bedding and for stripping to get pith for wicks for rush lights. Until 1725 grouse had been caught either by hawking or netting but now they were being shot.

The food in the farmhouses consisted mainly of oatcake, porridge and broths. A kail pot (a large flat cast-iron pan with a lid) stood on the hearth and was used for boiling water and as an oven for baking. In 1790 simple kitchen ranges were brought in with side ovens of cast-iron and water boilers.

There were a number of weavers in the district—we find three mentioned in deeds: William Banks of Ilton, John Imeson, William Banks.[6]

A tourist who visited Masham described the market place as being 'uncommonly spacious, built on three sides, but the houses so low and mean, that it has the appearance of a deserted place. The church is at the end of the fourth side, remarkably neat'. Another story tells how many of the houses were low, thatched buildings, with their eaves nearly reaching to the ground, whilst their ridges—which were constructed of green turf—mounted up to a very great height, so that the sheep (which were then shown at the September fairs, and were much wilder and more active on the leg than those now shown) used to take bounds and leaps and run upon the roofs of the houses, and gambol about upon them in such a very extraordinary manner as to present quite a spectacle to the gaping beholders below, and not a little bewilderment to their no less noisy canine companions.[7] The look of the square was beginning to change and in 1762 there is an agreement made between William Danby and Matthew Ward, who is thought to have built the stables at Swinton, to build some houses on the south side of the square adjoining on the east the inn lately occupied by Charles Hird. William Danby paid Ward £250 towards building them and he also paid William Beckwith £80 for building houses in North Street, Masham.[8]

Houses on the South side of Masham Square

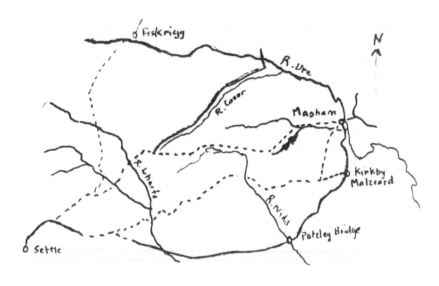

Sketch map of drove and market roads coming to Masham

Cloth makers with their packhorses (*Costume of Yorkshire, 1814*)

As can be seen from the map, drove and market roads went through Masham.[9] Market traders travelled these roads with packhorses carrying their wares. For some the signpost to Kettlewell on Pott Moor may have been the last they saw, for if they stopped for the night at the inn on Dead Man's Hill they were very likely not to wake again. A couple who kept this inn murdered their visitors during the night, pocketing their money and setting their horses loose on the moor. After a while the number of wild horses aroused the suspicions of the neighbourhood and more than 25 bodies were discovered—hence the name. There were also shorter tracks linking villages and outlying hamlets; these were used by 'badgers'—small traders licensed to carry corn from the markets to sell to individual customers or in other markets. They gave the name 'badger' to some of the tracks they used and we have Badger Lane in Masham which is the road to Grewelthorpe.

In 1732 there was a great flood and the wooden bridges at Masham and Tanfield were washed away. The present bridge was built in 1755; it was nearly swept away by another flood on 2 February 1822.

Mr Fisher tells us of an incident in Masham in 1745 during the Scottish Rebellion:

The good people of Mashamshire were thrown into a great state of alarm by a report that the young Pretender had gained a great victory over the English army [probably the battle of Falkirk] and that the Scots' army was advancing rapidly towards this neighbourhood. Panic-struck they immediately started to hide all their precious possessions in the most extraordinary places and in the most ludicrous manner, not forgetting themselves, in the best way they were able. After the danger was past the many ridiculous scenes which the panic gave rise to were much talked of and were remembered by the name of 'Runaway Wednesday'.

Masham bridge drawn by N. Whittock and engraved by J. Shury 1830

In the month of January 1741 a contested election took place for the representation of the County of York in Parliament. The following extracts taken from the poll book on that occasion give us the names of the people who were freeholders within Mashamshire at that date:

Freeholders names	Freehold	Place of abode	Candidate
Thomas Banks	Masham	Masham	Chomley and Turner
Joseph Calvert	Grewelthorpe	Masham	Turner
Thomas Fownes	Masham Parish	Masham Parish	Turner
Christopher Gardiner	Masham	Masham	Turner
Thomas Jackson	Masham Parish	Masham	Turner
John Lonsdale	Bellerby	Masham	Turner
William Lupton	Skipton	Masham	Turner
Matthew Metcalfe (schoolmaster)	Nidderdale	Masham	Turner
William Thirkhill	Galphay	Masham	Turner
John Wrather	Masham	Masham	Turner
Peter Young	Kirkby Malzeard	Masham	Turner

Nutwith Cote must have been quite a substantial manor house at this time; there is a large dovecote there which dates back to this century. The lords of a manor bred pigeons to provide themselves with meat. In 1769 Catherine Bartlett married John Ascough and in 1788 it went to the Pickersgill family. Mr Fisher talks of a comb manufactory at Nutwith but there seems to be no other record of this.

In 1713 James Metcalfe sold the Old Hall (now Park House), sometimes called Paradise House, to Abstrupus Danby along with two fields called Paradise or Paddock Sykes. In 1740 the Old Hall was converted into a barn and farmed by Widow Robinson for 13s per annum.[10]

The following are some of the byelaws passed by the Masham Manor Court:[11]

No-one shall lay anything that is noysum in the streets nor wash them in the town's wells.
No-one shall tether horses on the Sabbath or night time on town fields.
No-one shall use a mill out of the manor of Masham.
Swine must be kept rung.
Water courses must be kept scoured.
Geese and swine were not to be put on Town Pasture without taking gates:

Some of the fines were:

1s for throwing rubbish into the street
1s 6d for having broken fences
6s for an assault
1s for running unrung pigs in the town streets.

A town swineherd was still employed and in 1712 John Wardrope was appointed to 'drive swine for our town of Masham according to ancient custom'.

Nutwith Cote farmhouse

During this century it seems the church had fallen into disrepair and a lot of repairs were necessary; a number of them were undertaken by William Danby. In 1766 six new bells were purchased from James Harrison a local bell-founder.

William Danby was the largest contributor to the establishing and founding of the Grammar and Free Schools in Masham in 1760. A new school-house was built in 1753 for a cost of £105 19s, and the mason was paid £46 19s 6d. The school consisted of a headmaster who taught any children whose parents were prepared to pay, and an assistant master who taught thirty-five poor children free, and these were paid for by money left by Oswald Coates and Isabel Beckwith (her money was left to pay for the education of five poor boys of the name of Beckwith). A school in Colsterdale was also founded in 1787 and although there do not seem to be any records to show who was responsible it seems very probable that William Danby also founded this.

As wheeled traffic increased some of the more important roads were 'turnpiked'. This entailed an act of Parliament setting up a number of local people as trustees empowered to levy tolls in order to improve and keep up a length of road. In 1755 a turnpike road between Masham and Thirsk was set up. There were also plans to make a turnpike road from Masham via Ilton and Ramsgill to Grassington but this never materialised.

Horse trainer (*Costume of Yorkshire, 1814*)

Horseraces were held on the Marfield and the following are some of the articles agreed on regarding them:

Articles Agreed upon and concluded by Sir Abstrupus Danby knt. Sir Roger Beckwith Bart. Abstrupus Danby Esqr. John Dodsworth Esqr. Thomas Johnson John Beckwith John Bartlett gentlemen and others as followeth:–

1. It is agreed on that there shall be run for at Masham a Plate of five pounds value by any Horse Mare or Gelding not exceeding the value of Ten pounds upon friday the ninth day of September in the year of our Lord 1709 Between the hours of Twelve and Two a clock in the afternoon of the same day.

2. It is Agreed that no horse Mare or Gelding shall Run where the founders or any one of them will give upwards of Ten pounds in ready money for the same to the Owner thereof before the Running of the said Race, the said horse Mare or Gelding first to be delivered to the Buyer and he to pay downe the money at ye same time.

3. It is agreed that the said Plate shall be run for in a Place called the Marrfield situate within the Township of Masham aforesaid Three Heats each Heat Twice about leaving all the Posts upon the Right hand. And each Ryder to be Ten stone weight without the saddle and Bridle. And he that is adjudged to have the best of the said Three Heats shall have the Plate delivered him at Michael Jaques House in Masham aforesaid.

There were a number of further articles regarding the method of judging and the entry fee and weighing in.

William Danby had married Mary Affleck and when he died in 1781 he was succeeded by his eldest son William who was then 29. He was made High Sheriff of the North Riding in 1784 which proved to be a difficult job due to the state of the country following the treaty of peace ending the American War of Independence, and elections took place in the midst of fierce agitation for parliamentary reform. Having served his term as High Sheriff he set off, late in 1786, with his wife (née Caroline Seymour) on a Grand Tour in a secondhand travelling coach bought for the journey for £112 18s 6d. They returned to Swinton in October 1790 with a large number of works of art which they had bought on their tour.

The next year he started building on to his house but as most of his improvements at Swinton run into the nineteenth century I will deal with them all in the next chapter.

The open-field village was basically a self-contained unit. Cereals, meat, vegetables and beer were produced here. Pasture was needed for stock in summer and meadow for hay in winter. Meadow was divided up by lines which were trodden out annually or were allotted to tenants for the year, and areas were first divided into sixteenths each subdivided into quarters. Open arable lands were divided into two or three large 'fields' working either the two or three-field system of crop rotation. Fields were subdivided roughly into rectangular areas, made up of a number of sections known as strips. Outside arable and open meadow land was the common and waste land. This was used for cow or horse pasture, for plough cattle or for animals such as geese, swine or donkeys which were not legally given grazing land. Some land was left for gravel pits or for turf cutting, and wooded areas were retained for taking timber for fuel or repairs to buildings.

Over the years land was gradually enclosed; as some of this was done rather high-handedly during the eighteenth century it was decided to give it a more legal basis. It was realised that the land could be farmed more efficiently if it was divided up and enclosed. Private acts of Parliament were passed to effect the enclosure of a district. Commissioners were appointed to survey the parish and reallot the open lands in it among the farmers who had previously farmed it under the open-field system. The enclosure award of Mashamshire was the result of the 1790 private Act of Parliament, under which William Danby received by far the largest allotments although these consisted mostly of the poorer land. There were 29 allotments made in Masham township; the largest, of 431 acres, went to William Danby and the smallest, of 1 rood and 1 perch, to Robert Sympson Esquire. Those who received allotments were responsible for fencing them and some of the poorer farmers who got the smallest allotments were not able to afford this and sold out to the larger landowners. William Danby planted woods on several of his allotments as well as constructing a number of roads. This led to the look of the landscape as we now know it.

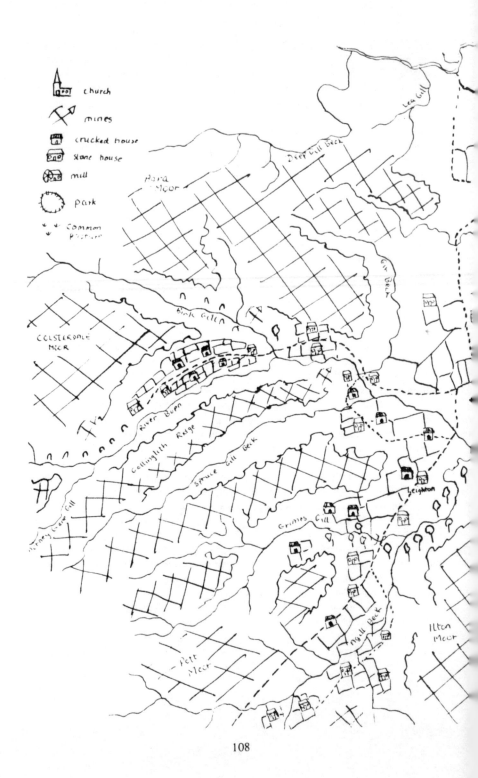

church

mines

crucked house

stone house

mill

park

common pasture

Lea Gill

Deer Gill Beck

Para Moor

Gill Beck

Birk Gill

COLSTERDALE MOOR

River Burn

Collingleth Ridge

Spruce Gill Beck

Leighton

Grimes Gill

Ingall Beck

Ilton Moor

Pott Moor

108

River Yore

N
↑

Low Ellington

Ellingstring

High Ellington

Swinney Beck

Fearby

Healey

River Yore

Colsterdale mill

Masham

River Burn

Burn

Sole Beck

Swinton

Eller Beck

Northern marshes

Den Beck

River Yore

Ilton

Outline map of the district during the eighteenth century

Miss Elizabeth Danby (sister of William Danby) by Henry Pickering 1768 (Swinton collection)

The following are some housekeeping expenses of the 1780s:[12]

1 doz lemons		2s	4d
Hindquarters of lamb		5s	6d
1 doz oranges		2s	4d
2 chickens		5s	6d
Week's washing		2s	
4 concert tickets	£1	1s	
Coachman's breeches	£1	1s	
Coachman's boots	£1	1s	
Music at Mr Danby's ball	£15		
2 pairs of shoes		9s	
Indian silk for nightgown	£2	5s	
2 dolls	£1	4s	6d
False hair		5s	
Given to a boy for a bullfinch's nest		1s	

The following are some extracts from an old book which Mr and Mrs Carter and Mr A. Taylor found with other papers on a ledge in an old chimney in College Grove:

Q. A thing with a thundering breech,
I weighing a thoufand Pounds welly;
  I have heard it roar
  Louder than Guy's wild Boar:
They fay it had Death in its Belly.

A. *It is a Cannon.*

Q. It flies without wings
Between filken ftrings,
And leaves, as you'll find,
The guts ftill behind.

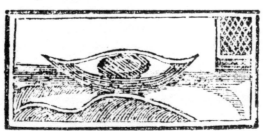

A. *It is a Weaver's Shuttle.*

Q. Clofe in a Cage a bird I keep,
  That fings both day and night;

When other birds are faſt aſleep,
  It's notes yield ſweet delight.

A. *It is a Clock.*

Q. Tho' to the green wood,
    Full oft hath it gang'd,
Yet yields us no good,
    'Till decently hang'd.

A. *It is a Hog fatten'd with Acorns, which
makes good Bacon when hang'd a drying.*

Q. There was a fair Maid,
    Who merrily ſaid,
Her lover was ſtupid and dull:

Q. My ears they run round about,
And reach to the ground,
To the admiration of a man;
The one part is dead,
The other well fed;
This Riddle expound if you can.

A. *It is a Horse and Cart; the Wheels betoken Ears that reach the Ground; the Horse is fed; the Cart is dead.*

Q. I'm carry'd thro' the city,
Seeming mighty pretty,
No quarrel or wrangle I breed:
My body is taper,
I fear not a rapier,
Tho' stabb'd not a drop do I bleed.

A. *'Tis the Scabbard of a Sword.*

Q. My skin is black, my blood is sweet,
My heart resembles wood,
In which there's something may be eat,
Tho' not exceeding good.

A. *A Black Chery.*

Q. My back is broad, my belly is thin,
   And I am fent to pleafure a youth,
Where mortal man has never been,
   Tho' ftrange, it is a naked truth.

A. *A Paper Kite, which mounts the lofty Air.*

Q. 'Tis neither flefh nor bone
   Yet it paffes on ;
By which is fairly fhewn
   The length and breadth of man.

A. *A Man's Shadow, whilft he is walking in the Sun.*

Q. From five feet high,
   Up to the sky,
It reaches, tho' 'tis round :
   Now try your wits,
   If fancy hits,
This Riddle you'll expound.

A. *The Sight of a Man's Eye.*

12 1800

William Danby by John Jackson R.A. (Swinton collection)

Life in Mashamshire at this time was influenced a great deal by the personality of the owner of Swinton and Lord of the Manor, William Danby. By all accounts he was a fascinating and delightful man and spent twenty to thirty years making Swinton into a rich expression of picturesque ideas. When he returned from his grand tour in 1790 he began building on to Swinton and improving the grounds. At first he thought of building a house on the site of Low Mains but decided against it. His first extension to Swinton was a wing to the west which included the drawing room which was designed by James Wyatt.

The South front of Swinton Park about 1815–20

William Danby's drawing-room, decorated by James Wyatt about 1793–4

William Danby's museum under construction in 1813–14

Swinton Park when it had been castellated

He also built a large wing to the north to connect the house to the stables. In 1813 he built on another wing to the west of the drawing room consisting of a library to house his books and a museum for his geological, botanical, archaeological and other collections. He consulted Lugar over the building of the museum and was persuaded by him to turn the house into a castle. This was done between 1821 and 1824 when a massive tower, turrets, battlements and a new billiards room and library were added to the north and south sides of the original house. He also continued the improvements to the park and grounds at Swinton. In 1810 he had more or less finished his improvements to the southern chain of lakes and a start was made on the northern lakes. Rocks were set at the edge of Top Lake and a projection was made in Coffin Lake. Massive embankments were needed along one side of Top Lake and at the ends of Coffin Lake. In 1811 work was started on Quarry Gill Bridge. The lower part was built by Mickle and the upper part was designed by Foss and it took eight years to build at a cost of £11 000. Each stone is numbered with Roman numerals.

Quarry Gill Bridge by Anne Danby

William Danby was also a great patron of the arts and in about 1804 Ibbetson, who had been given an introduction to him, was commissioned to paint some pictures of Swinton and Masham.

William Danby built the Druid's Temple at Ilton about 1800. At this time there was a great interest in druids and William Danby, having seen a similar but original temple on his tour of the Continent, decided to build a copy at Ilton in one of the enclosures he had just been granted and was planting up.

As well as being a very amiable and generous man he was also an accomplished scholar with a great knowledge of literature, science, geology and mineralogy. He was an excellent player of the violoncello and had a complete set of stringed instruments for the use of his friends. The Danbys were a very hospitable couple and entertained many distinguished friends. In 1806 Master Betty, the boy actor who was well known on the London stage, visited Swinton and in 1807 John Raphael Smith came and painted a very good likeness of Julius Caesar Ibbetson when he was there.

Julius Caesar Ibbetson by John Raphael Smith

Druids Temple

Archery Meeting at Swinton by R. Metcalfe (Swinton collection)

William Danby with his gun by Julius Caesar Ibbetson

Masham Fair by Julius Caesar Ibbetson (Swinton collection)

Gossips at the Well by Julius Caesar Ibbetson

The Woodcutter by Julius Caesar Ibbetson (Williamson Gallery, Birkenhead)

The Broomseller, Swinton Village by Julius Caesar Ibbetson

When he first met the Danbys Ibbetson said: 'The world ought to be peopled with such folks'. When he first came to live in Masham he stayed at the King's Head Hotel, leaving his wife in the Lake District, but he found this rather expensive and, having persuaded William Danby to commission a further six paintings, he moved his family to Masham.

According to his biography he lodged with a Mrs Powell. On a list of inhabitants of Masham in 1801 there is a Mr Caleb Powell living on the corner of Park St and Chapman Lane so this may have been where he lived. He was popular in Masham as he was a good, sociable and kindhearted man. He was amongst those forerunners of the District Council who took responsibility for road development. It is said when he had finished a painting and wanted an honest opinion of it he would put it in the window of his house when the schoolchildren passed by, leaving the window open to hear what their comments were. One of his paintings is of a broomseller in Swinton village, showing a girl wearing a summerlike straw bonnet. The making of these was for many years a local industry in Masham. The broomseller went round the villages crying 'There's a large one for the lady—and a small one for the baby—Come! Buy a broom off me!' or 'Old boots or shoes I'll take for brooms; Come buy, to make clean all your rooms'.[1]

Children at Play by Julius Caesar Ibbetson

Root House.

Arns Gill.

Swinton Park. Yorkshire

First Lake.

Quarry Gill.

Local views by George Cuitt

Another artist of this time who came to live in Masham was George Cuitt. He did a series of etchings of the Abbeys of Yorkshire as well as of many other old buildings and castles. He also painted a number of views of Masham and Swinton.

Another inhabitant of Masham who later rose to fame during this century was William Jackson who was born at Masham Mill in 1815. His father was a miller at Tanfield but as there was no doctor there his mother came to live at Masham Mill until the baby was born. From an early age he showed great interest in music. His father was a bellringer, chorister and fife-player in the Masham Volunteers. Young William would walk with his father every Sunday from Tanfield to Masham where he because a chorister. It was probably on these walks that he developed his love of nature which was to show in his music. He started his schooling at Tanfield but was later sent to a boarding-school in Pateley Bridge. At 13 he went back home to work at the mill with his father. He had to drive a donkey-cart laden with flour and meal round the countryside trying to get new business; he also helped his father on the farm. He took part in various sports, he was a very good swimmer and according to his biography his diving feats off Masham bridge were often watched by a throng of admirers (the river must have been a great deal deeper or else this must be rather a tall story!). He became conductor of a newly formed band in Masham and walked from Tanfield twice a week to the practices. It was then that he started writing music and he played all the instruments in the band when needed. In about 1832 Mr Danby gave a pipe organ to Masham church and William Jackson became the organist. In 1839 he became a partner with Mr Ascough, a tallow chandler in Masham, and moved to Masham. His family lived at Mill House, Masham for many years. He now began to write music in earnest. He had considerable success and soon became well known especially for his oratories 'Deliverance of Israel from Babylon' and 'Isaiah'. In 1852 he took over a firm of piano-makers and dealers in Bradford. He continued to write music including much church music, songs and glees. He became conductor of Bradford Choral Union, and choirmaster at Bradford Festivals.[2]

Masham and the moors by George Cuitt

William Danby throughout his life was a great benefactor to the town of Masham. He contributed generously to many charities and a lot of the good that he did shall never be known as he did it quietly and often secretly. He did much to restore and improve the church including most of the cost of repairing the steeple after it was blown down by a gale. This was done without any scaffolding by a Mr Wooton of Nottingham who fastened ladders to the side of the steeple with iron clamps and took down the damaged part of the steeple, built it up again and fixed the vane upon it. For this he was paid £28 15s 10d. Mr Danby also paid for the organ and an endowment of £30 a year to be paid to the organist. With a Mr W. Heslington, Mr Danby built Healey school and schoolmaster's house at Kell Bank and endowed it with a stipend for the schoolmaster. This was done between 1820 and 1822.

At the beginning of the century, during the French war Napoleon threatened to invade England and volunteer corps were raised throughout the country. In Masham more than 100 men volunteered providing the cost of their own uniform and other necessary equipment. William Danby and Timothy Hutton of Clifton Castle were their leaders. In 1804 they were called up for permanent duty at Richmond and the inns there often echoed to the song of the Masham Volunteers:

We Volunteers of Masham, our clothing is of red,
And if we meet the Frenchmen we'll make them us to dread;
Our clothing is of red, my boys, and turned up with black,
But if we meet those French boys we'll make their bones to crack.

And with Danby we will go, will go,
With Danby we will go;
For Hutton is a soldier's friend,
And that we all do know.

Mr Fisher tells us the following about the Volunteers:

The Mashamshire volunteers were a fine body of men and were all ready to go to war to defend their country. Early one morning, the people of Masham were aroused by the ringing of the bells, the beat of drums, and the call, 'To arms—to arms'. News ran like wildfire that the beacon-fires were lit up, and that the French were coming. Presently Mr Danby and Mr Hutton were seen bustling about the town, and the men were under arms and in marching order. The baggage waggons were got ready as by a magic spell and all were soon on the march towards the Eastern coast, ready to give the enemy a meeting on his attempting a landing on our shores. There was a great bustle and rush in Masham on that memorable morning, with wives and sweethearts bidding their men goodbye and the men marching off ready 'to do or die' in their country's cause. However when they got to Thirsk they found that the beacon fires had been lit by a mistake and a halt was called that they might have something to eat and drink before they went home. They celebrated very well and managed to stagger home much to the relief of their wives. The Loyal Dales Volunteers had also mustered owing to the mistake and their gallant conduct came to the notice of Parliament where a vote of thanks was passed calling attention to their zeal and services in protecting their country from the threatened invasion. At the conclusion of the peace their muskets were sold and the money was given to the Free school of Masham.

128

Masham Volunteers in Masham Square by Julius Caesar Ibbetson

Extracts from the instruction book for the Masham Volunteers now part of the Cunliffe-Lister papers in Bradford Central Library

PLATOON EXERCISE

PLATOON EXERCISE

In 1833 William Danby died at the age of 82 and his death was greatly mourned by his many tenants and especially the poor to whom he had always been a kind and sympathetic friend. The following extracts from the diary of Timothy Hutton Esq. of Clifton Castle tell us something of this:

Wed. 4th December 1833 William Danby died at Swinton, he was to me a sincere friend and excellent neighbour and though upwards of 80 years of age I cannot but deplore the loss of as truly good and truly benevolent man as he was.

Friday 13th December 1833 Went to Swinton at one o'clock and attended as mourner the funeral of my much lamented friend William Danby. Sir Robert Affleck, Miss Salmon, Mr Thompson, Mr Tucker, Mr Mouson, Mr Preston, T. Hutton and Col. Dutton were the mourners in the order placed. The tenants on horseback in threes to the number of 80 before the Hearse and 6 horses followed the mourning coaches, Gentlemen's carriages of the Neighbours 19—the Labourers 60 on foot—the day was favourable and the whole passed off as well as could possibly be wished.

He did not have any children and he left the estate to his second wife Ann Danby for her life. In 1838 she married Admiral Harcourt who then became Lord of the Manor. He became a Justice of the Peace and was appointed High Sheriff of the County of York in 1848. He and Mrs Danby-Harcourt, as she became known, did a great deal for Masham although they only had a life interest in the estate. They built twelve almshouses, a school and schoolhouse in Swinton Road and a church

Schoolhouse in Swinton Road

Healey church

and vicarage in Healey. They also contributed very largely to the restoration of Masham church and to the improvement of both the Grammar and Free school. They also owned racehorses and one, Ellington, won the Derby in 1856 in the slowest time on record.

The following are some items from Mrs Danby's housekeeping book of the 1820s and 1830s:

200 crawfish	6s 0d
2 quarts cranberries	4s 0d
6 lbs salmon	10s 6d
60 oysters	3s 0d
3 chickens at 1s 3d each	3s 9d

A typical week's housekeeping account of 1837 is:

Washer woman	2s 0d
Jane Hill 2 days at 9d a day	1s 6d
3 quarts of cream 1s 6d a quart	4s 6d
Brooms for the house	2s 0d
12 pounds of honey at 1s 3d a lb	15s 0d
2 pair of soap at 3s 6d each	7s 0d
Cream cheese	2s 0d
Richmond butter bill	15s 6d
Grocer's bill	£1 5s 6d
Butcher bill	£9 1s 7d

This would have been for a household of approximately 20.

Almshouses in Swinton Road

135

Masham school

The school-house used by the Grammar school was first built by William Danby and was improved by Admiral Harcourt. The school-house belonging to the Free school was originally built by William Danby but was afterwards pulled down and rebuilt by Mrs Danby-Harcourt in 1834. She also built additional rooms to house a school for girls to be taught needlework and for pupils attending the Infant school which was added to the Free School.

The following were Mrs Danby's rules for the schoolmistress in 1818:

Mrs Danby agrees to give Mrs Dobson ten guineas a year upon condition she attends to, and executes the following rules:

To teach twenty children, boys and girls when there are that number from the age of three years and a half old until they are employed by Mr Prest or are of an age approved by Mrs Danby.
To teach both boys and girls to spell, read, sew and knit also to teach them their prayers and catechism.
To lead prayers before school begins and again at night before the children go home.

School to begin at 8 o'clock in the morning, break up at 12 o'clock, begin again at 1 o'clock and break up at 4 o'clock from the first day of November to the first day of March.

School to begin at 8 o'clock in the morning, break up at 12 o'clock, begin again at 2 o'clock and break up at 6 o'clock from the first day of March till the first day of November.

The children to be dismissed for the day upon Saturday at 12 o'clock.

The children to be assembled, and walk two and two to church, a quarter of an hour before the service begins every Sunday morning and again in the afternoon when the weather permits.

The girls are to make a curtsey and the boys a bow going into and leaving the school.

The mistress to have three week's holiday at hay-time and three weeks at harvest.

The mistress to be neat and clean in her person.

Her rules for parents and children were:

The children to be in school every morning at 8 o'clock, leave it at 12 o'clock, meet again at 1 o'clock and leave it at 4 o'clock, from the first of November till the first of March.

The children to be in school every morning at 8 o'clock, leave it at 12 o'clock, meet again at 2 o'clock and leave it at 6 o'clock from the 1st March until the 1st November.

The children to have their heads combed, hands and face washed every morning and evening before they go to school.

The children are to be made clean and neat every Sunday morning and afternoon, and to be at school at 10 o'clock to accompany the mistress to church.

The parents are to submit to any punishment Mr Prest and the mistress may think proper to inflict—in case they do not the children will be turned out.

In 1821 the headmaster of the Grammar school received £51 14s a year over and above what he was paid by the parents of the children he taught, while the master of the Charity school received £24 12s for the teaching of thirty-five children who were educated free. But this was changed and the payments for both masters was made more equal. The management of the school was made over to a body of trustees who declared that the Grammar school should be open to the children of all resident inhabitants of the parish of Masham and that the instructions should be in the principles of the Christian religion, the Greek, Latin and French languages, mathematics, algebra, arithmetic, general English literature and composition, sacred and profane history, geography, reading, writing, and also such other languages, arts, and sciences as the trustees may deem expedient. They also declared that the Free school should be open to the children of all resident inhabitants of the parish of Masham, between the ages of seven and sixteen years, who should be able to read words of one syllable and should be admitted in order of application. They should be taught reading, writing, spelling, English grammar, arithmetic, and such subjects of general and useful knowledge as may from time to time be directed, or authorised by the Committee of Council of Education. In 1841 there were about eighty boys in the Grammar school.

The first Methodist Chapel

In 1791 the Reverend William Lawson became vicar of Masham and Kirkby Malzeard. During the war with France he had been held prisoner there, and when peace was declared and he was released he built himself a vicarage in Kirkby Malzeard and lived the life of a recluse. Due to his neglect of the parish many branches of the new religions of this period were started up in Masham. Masham Wesleyans started meeting in a cottage at Moorheads. They later moved to Masham, first to Common Head, the house of Roger Kirkbride, and then to the old Court House Chamber in College Lane holding services alternately with the Baptists. Their first chapel was built in 1817 in Chapel Lane (now Morton Row) on land given by Christopher Durham. We can see from the following entries in his niece's diary how this came about:

27th May 1817
This day I have been pleading with my uncle for a piece of land on which to build a chapel at Masham and, praise the Lord, the work is his. I have succeeded.

9th June 1817
My old uncle [then 76] and I, went to solicit Mr Danby's favour to permit us to build a Chapel, and we were denied, after a parley about an hour long, on the principles of Methodism. The day before, I said I was willing to be sent anywhere. This was a very great cross to go to Mr Danby's. Yet then I was willing to bear it; though I acknowledge I never felt anything so hard to do; and now, after I am disappointed, I feel it harder to be resigned.

We also learn from her diaries that there were one hundred and seventy children attending the Sunday School each Sunday. One child learnt one hundred and twenty verses of Psalm 119 in one week, another child of seven knew three hundred and thirty verses. Her first husband died eighteen months after they were married and she later lived in the house next to the chapel and took the Sunday School. In 1892 the Methodists built their present chapel on land sold to them by Lord Masham.

Methodism was especially popular among the farmers and workers who felt it was more their kind of religion, while that of the established church had always belonged to the upper classes. Money was raised in the villages to build their own chapels. Ellingstring Chapel was rebuilt in 1848, Fearby Chapel in 1849, Ilton in 1876 (costing upwards of £200) and Ellington in 1877 (costing upwards of £300). Miss Jackson remembers her mother telling her how her grandfather, Mr Wrather of Fearby, led the stone for the Fearby chapel from a quarry on Howe Hill with the women helping by carrying the stone in their aprons.

The Society of Friends—'The Quakers'—had a meeting-house in Masham, which at one time was the house on the corner of College Lane and Black Bull Lane. They also had a burial-ground at Ellington; this was very much a Quaker village as they had a tannery there and there were quite a number of their houses along the side of the road between the village and the main road. These were demolished at the end of the century. Quaker Terrace in Masham was so named because the Quaker family of Rowantree built a dairy there.

The Baptists were the next to come; they held their meetings in the lobby in the long room connected to the Bay Horse Inn and then the Old Court Chamber. Afterwards they bought a site in Grewelthorpe Road and built a chapel in 1822.

The Primitive Methodists and the Reform Wesleyans also had branches. The former built their chapel in Silver Street (the present Post Office).

In 1833 Reverend Waddington took over from Mr Lawson, and after the many years of neglect there was a great deal for him to do in the parish. As well as reorganising the school he built a vicarage in Masham which is said to have cost him a considerable amount more than the grants which he received.

The present Methodist Chapel

139

The first vicarage now Glebe House

He was a Fellow of Trinity College and wrote a History of the Chuch. He was very liberal in his attitude to the Nonconformist parishioners. He subscribed 2 guineas a year to their Sunday School, and at the Bazaar to raise money to build their chapel he provided children's clothes for one of the stalls. He became Dean of Durham in 1840 and Reverend Thomas Riddell took over from him; he proved to be a very good and popular vicar. He was one of the founders and first President of the Masham Mechanics Institute which was founded in 1848. Its objectives were the provision of a comfortable reading-room, well supplied with newspapers, periodicals, and suitable books to which, according to Mr Fisher, 'the young men in the town might resort in an evening, in preference to spending their time at the street corners, or at the alehouses'. It proved a great success, the only problem being the want of a suitable building. In September 1855 Mr Riddell died suddenly and this caused much regret to his many friends in Masham. They decided they would like to erect some memorial of him in Masham and as he had taken such interest in the Mechanics Institute it was decided to raise the money to build a house for it and to name it after him. This was done and the public opening took place on 3 November 1856. It now houses the Midland Bank.

The Harcourts were not the only local racehorse owners; Captain Wrather raised a small but valuable stud of racehorses, which went to his brother on his death, whereupon Nutwith won the St Leger in 1842 and Miss Lydia and the Maid of Masham also won several other important stakes. The Wrather family lived at Bank Villa and were responsible for building the Grotto at Burton. Captain Wrather's father, the Reverend John Wrather, was a wag and a poet and wrote the following poem to Johnnie Knubley the famous barber of Masham drawn by Ibbetson:

The Spiral Pole from far was seen,
To tell the world that there
Frail man might lose his lengthen'd beard,
In Johnnie's Elbow-chair;
Their shatter'd heads with age grown hoar
Or robb'd of hair in vain,
But Johnnie can their loss restore,
And make them young again.

Johnnie Knubley the barber of Masham drawn by
Julius Caesar Ibbetson

We can get some idea of what Masham was like in 1840 from the following entry in Pigot's Gazetteer of that date:

MASHAM AND NEIGHBOURHOOD

Masham is a small market town and parish—the latter partly in the liberty of St. Peter, York, but chiefly in the eastern division of the wapentake of Hang, North Riding; 34 miles N.W. from York, 17 S. from Richmond, 17 N.W. from Boroughbridge, 6 S. from Bedale, and 10 S.E. from Middleham. The town is delightfully situated on the western bank of the river Ure, and the adjacent country is abundantly fertile. In addition to agricultural pursuits, numbers of men are employed in the combing of wool, some of the females in manufacturing a coarse straw plat for hats, and at a distance of about half a mile is an extensive flax mill, which affords occupation to many others. A court leet is held annually, at which a constable is appointed—the jurisdiction of the court also extending to the recovery of debts under 40s.

The church, dedicated to St. Mary, is a small but handsome edifice, in the English style of architecture, with a tower surmounted by a lofty and elegant spire: the benefice is a vicarage, with that of Kirkby-Malzeard, in the patronage of the master and fellows of Trinity college, Cambridge: the present incumbent is the Rev. Thomas Riddell. There are places of worship for baptists and Wesleyan methodists. The grammar school here was founded by William Danby, Esq., in 1760; there are about eighty boys, who are all stipendiary pupils: there is a free school, likewise, for boys and girls. This place was anciently the residence of the baronial family of Scroop, to which belonged Henry, Lord le Scroop, lord treasurer, and Archbishop Scroop, both beheaded for high treason in the reign of Henry IV.—The market, which is held on Wednesday, has of late years been but thinly attended: the fairs are on the 17th and 18th September, and during the spring every alternate Monday, for sheep and cattle. The parish of Masham contained, in 1831, 2995 inhabitants: and of that number 1276 were returned for the township.

POST OFFICE, Market-place, George Jackson, Post Master.—Letters from London and all parts arrive every day at twelve, and are despatched every afternoon at one.

GENTRY AND CLERGY

Barker Mr Edmund, Park st	Lightfoot Mrs. Grace, Park st
Bolland Mr Roger, Market place	M'Kay Rev. David, Silver st
Bowes Miss Cecilia, Park st	Martin Mrs —, Market place
Dalton Capt. John, Slanyforth grange	Milbank Mark, esq. Thorpe hall
Dalton Col. John, Slanyforth hall	Riddell Rev. Thomas, Vicarage
Harcourt Capt. O. V. Swinton park	Thompson Mr. James, Silver st
Hutton Darcey, esq. Aldborough hall	Watson Mrs —, Park row
Hutton Timothy, esq. Clifton castle	Wrather Mr Samuel, Silver st
	Wrather Capt. Thos. Market place

142

ACADEMIES & SCHOOLS

FREE SCHOOL (boys') Market place—Christopher Marsden master

FREE SCHOOL (girls) Park row—Mary Belshaw, mistress

GRAMMAR SCHOOL (day & boarding) Market place—Edmund Barker, master

Stubbs Ann, Park st

Wilkinson Jane, Park st

ATTORNEYS

Calvert John, Silver st

Prest John (and agent to the Yorkshire fire & life office), Silver st

BLACKSMITHS

Beckwith William, Silver st

Fleetham Matthew (and cut nail manufacturer), Park st

Imeson George, Swinton

Mallaby Peter, Back st

Metcalfe John, Park st

Rider Robert, Park st

Ward Peter, Park st

BOOT AND SHOE MAKERS

Benson John, Burn lane

Brewster James, Park row

Court Thomas, Back st

Elsworth William, Silver st

Furby George, Market place

Haste John, Park st

Mainman John, Market place

Moor Joseph, Lobby

Myers Edward, Park st

Pybus Edward, Silver st

Sturdy Francis, Silver st

Towler Isaac, Back st

Towler Thomas, Lobby

Wharton Thomas, Park row

BREWERS AND MALTSTERS

Lightfoot William, Market place

Wood John, Silver st

BUTCHERS

Appleton George, Market place

Glew John, Fearby

Jackson John, Silver st

Williamson William (& cheese and bacon factor), Park row

Wood William, Hill

COOPERS

Duffield James, Back st

Duffield John, Park st

GROCERS AND DEALERS IN SUNDRIES

Clarkson Charlotte, Silver st

Carter Thomas, Market place

Graham James, Black Bull lane

Hawkin John, Market place

London William & Co. Market place

Raper Christopher, Silver st

Scurrah Mary, Black Bull lane

Thompson Robert, Lobby

Ward Peter, Park st

INNS AND PUBLIC HOUSES

Bay Horse, Thomas Irving, Silver st

Bull Inn, John Wood, Silver st

George & Dragon, Thos. Hanley, Hill

King's Head (and posting house), John Lightfoot, Market place

King's Head, William Scorer, Fearby

Lord Nelson Inn, Thos. Hammond, Market place

Mason's Arms, Sarah Clarkson, Silver st

White Bear, John Teasdale, Silver st

IRONMONGERS

Jackson George, Market place

Terry William, Hill

JOINERS AND CABINET MAKERS

Alton William (and timber merchant), Back st

Fisher John, Park row

Metcalfe James, Market place

Towler John, Park st

LINEN AND WOOLLEN DRAPERS

Carter Thomas, Silver st

London William & Co. Market place

Raper John, Park st

MILLINERS AND DRESS MAKERS

Ascough Eliza, Park st

Beckwith Margaret, Silver st

Pratt Margaret, Market place

PAINTERS

Falkingham Thomas, Park st

Findlayson William, Market place

SADDLERS
London James, Market place
Stott Thomas, Market place

STONE MASONS
Clarkson Matthew, Silver st
Hall William, Park st

STRAW HAT MAKERS
Deighton Mary, Market place
Duffield Ann, Park st
Thompson Betty, Lobby

STRAW PLAT DEALERS
Scurrah Mary, Black Bull lane
Thompson Robert, Lobby

SURGEONS
Dalgliesh Wm.M. M.D. Market place
Hutchinson Richard Ella, Park st

TAILORS
Atkinson Henry, Park st
Castling Henry, Silver st
London Wm. & Co. (& drapers),
Market place
Thompson Robert, Back st
Towler Samuel, Black Bull lane

TALLOW CHANDLERS
Ascough & Jackson, Park st
Carter Thomas, Market place

WATCH AND CLOCK MAKERS
Pratt William, Market st
Terry William, Hill

WHEELWRIGHTS
Alton William, Park st
Atkinson Robert, Coilege lane
Fryer George, Park st
Sturdy John, Park st

WOOL COMBERS
Cummins John, Lobby
Jackson Edmund and Elizabeth,
near the Market place
Ruccroft James, Park row

WOOLSTAPLERS
Carter Thomas, Market place
Cummins John, Lobby
Williamson William, Park row

MISCELLANEOUS
Ascough Henry fellmonger, Park st
Backhouse Sarah, china and earthenware dealer, Silver st
Calvert George, plumber and glazier, Market place
Coldbeck Christopher, brazier and glazier, Lobby
Cuitt George, artist, Mount pleasant
Deighton John, hairdresser, Market place
Fryer George, confectioner, Park st
Hawkin John, chymist, druggist, and oil and colourman
Husband Wm. glove maker, Market place
Imeson and Carter, iron merchants, Silver st
Jackson Elizabeth, miller, Masham mill
Jackson Wm. professor of music, Park st
Prest James, flax dresser, &c. Burton mill
Pullen Thomas, coach builder, Silver st
Pybus William, baker, Park st
Roper Christopher, registrar of births and deaths, Masham
Theakston Robert, cattle dealer, Park st
Thwaites Richard, sieve maker, Park st
Wood John, wine and spirit merchant, Silver st

COACHES
To MIDDLEHAM, the *Highflyer* (from York), calls at the Lord Nelson Inn, every Tuesday, Thursday, and Saturday evening at eight.
To YORK, the *Highflyer* (from Middleham), calls at the Lord Nelson Inn, every Monday, Wednesday, and Friday morning at seven; goes through Ripon and Boroughbridge.

144

To BEDALE, Margaret Rayner, from her house, Market place, every Tuesday.
To LEEDS, John Nelson, from his house, Back st, every Monday.

To MIDDLEHAM, Margaret Rayner, her house, Market place, every Monday.
To RICHMOND, John Nelson, from his house, Back st, every Friday.

King's Head Hotel (detail from a painting by Julius Caesar Ibbetson)

From this we can also see that two stagecoaches passed through Masham calling at the Lord Nelson Inn. Railways were soon to bring the coaching era to an end. There was also a busy carrier trade. Carrier wagons came into being in about 1500, and they were the first public vehicles intended for the carriage of heavy goods and later for passengers as well. They travelled at a rate of about 3 mph which would have meant a three-hour journey to Ripon. The trip to Leeds took from 9 am Monday till 8 am Tuesday.

The King's Head was the most important inn. It was a posting house where travellers could hire and change horses on a journey. You could also hire a post-chaise (a two to four-seater carriage with a closed top) which was expensive but it was preferred by the ladies. It was also used as the Excise Office where taxes were collected on certain trades, such as hawkers and auctioneers, and licences were issued for carrying guns and keeping manservants, dogs, horses, and carriages. With the spread of the temperance movement in the 1850s the offices were moved away from inns.

In 1885 there were two temperance establishments in Masham. The temperance hotel and shop was at the west end of the Market Place on the north side of the Lord Nelson Inn and the temperance coffee house was on the corner of Red Lane and Park Square.

Occupations in Masham in 1851[3]

1 Vicar
1 Doctor
1 Solicitor
1 Accountant
2 Schoolmasters, 1 assistant
5 Schoolmistresses
1 Governess
1 Inland Revenue Officer
1 Baptist minister
1 Wesleyan minister
1 Primitive Methodist minister
 (in Ripon)
1 Curate in Healey
1 Teacher of singing
1 Teacher of music
1 Actress, 3 Actors 1 Proprietor
 (lodging)
3 Fundholders
5 Nurses
1 Midwife
1 Sexton
1 Master tailor
6 Tailors
15 Shoemakers
2 Basket-makers
2 Saddlers and 1 book-binder
17 Dressmakers
1 Rope-maker
1 Sieve and riddle-maker
1 Machine-maker
1 Bonnet-maker
3 Straw bonnet-makers
1 Cabinet maker and 1 apprentice
1 Umbrella-maker
1 Cooper and labourer
2 Broom and mat-makers
1 Watchmaker
1 Tinplate-maker and 1 labourer
1 Staymaker
1 Cutler
4 Coachbuilders
3 Coach-smiths
1 Coach-trimmer
2 Coach-painters
5 Carpenters
3 Plumbers and glaziers

4 Stonemasons
4 Joiners
11 Blacksmiths
1 Painter and paper-hanger
1 Skinner
26 Woolcombers
1 Wool-sorter
2 Wool-staplers
2 Flax-dressers
1 Flax-spinner
2 Hairdressers

1 Dealer in millinery
1 Dealer in earthenware
5 Grocers
3 Bakers
3 Butchers
1 Chemist and druggist
1 Confectioner
1 Ironmonger and Post Office
1 Linen and wool-draper
1 Post Office messenger
6 Innkeepers ⎫ Theakston and
3 Maltsters ⎬ Lightfoot did
3 Brewers and 3 labourers ⎭ all three
2 Tallow chandlers
1 Miller and 4 labourers
1 Flour-dealer
1 Butter-factor
1 Horse-trainer
2 Ostlers
2 Grooms
2 Errand boys
8 Farmers
51 Agricultural labourers
29 Carriers
2 Gardeners
1 Pig-dealer
4 Washer-women
2 Chelsea pensioners
58 House-servants
27 Paupers
170 Schoolchildren
19 Annuitants.

The cloth-dressers (*Costume of Yorkshire, 1814*)

The preemer boy (*Costume of Yorkshire, 1814*)

Occupations in the villages

Foxholme and Shaws
3 Farmers
1 Stonemason
1 Mantuamaker
1 Boot and shoemaker
1 Straw bonnet-maker
1 Woolcomber
1 Castrator
1 Joiner
1 Coach-smith app.

Swinton
1 Joiner
1 Carpenter
1 Land agent
1 Woolcomber
1 Shoemaker
1 Veterinary surgeon
1 Coachman
1 Footman
1 Gamekeeper
2 Tilemakers
1 Blacksmith
House staff
Farmers
Labourers

Ilton
3 Shoemakers
1 Stonemason
1 Carpenter
1 Tilemaker
1 Schoolmistress
1 Molecatcher
4 Dressmakers
1 Plough-maker
1 House-slater
Farmers
Labourers

Ellington
1 Grocer
3 Skinners
1 Dressmaker
1 Shoemaker
3 Carpenters
10 Farmers
15 Labourers

Ellingstring
3 Shoemakers
2 Blacksmiths
1 Tailor

1 Innkeeper
2 Grocers
1 Dressmaker
1 Carpenter
2 Boot and shoemakers
1 Schoolmaster
1 Schoolmistress
1 Hawker
1 Horsebreaker
1 Linen-draper
1 Beehive-maker
9 Farmers
21 Labourers

Colsterdale
14 Miners
1 Dressmaker
3 Innkeepers
1 Whitesmith and cutler
2 Stonemason
1 Blacksmith
1 Laundress
1 Shoemaker
7 Small farmers (some also miners)

Gownthley Foot
1 Blacksmith
7 Farmers
7 Labourers

Leighton
7 Farmers
5 Labourers
1 Slate and flag-mason
1 Gamekeeper
1 Stonemason

Healey and Sutton
1 Cattle dealer
1 Cornmiller
1 Shoemaker
3 Schoolmasters
1 Road-labourer
2 Tailors
1 Blacksmith
1 House-mason
1 Innkeeper
2 Carpenters
1 Butcher
7 Cotton mill-workers
9 Farmers
12 Labourers

Fearby
3 Carpenters
1 Shoemaker
6 Dressmakers
3 Grocers
2 Cordwainers and 1 app.
1 Tailor
2 Straw bonnet-makers
1 Horsebreaker
2 Schoolmistresses
3 Innkeepers
2 Blacksmiths
2 Joiners
1 Saddler
1 Sodawater-manufacturer
13 Farmers
23 Labourers

148

Line swinglers (*Costume of Yorkshire, 1814*)

Threshing at Shaws by Julius Caesar Ibbetson

In 1851 the first census in which people had to give their occupations was taken and, as can be seen from the list, the occupations were many and varied. A great many of these occupations have long since died out but brewing is one industry which still survives as a flourishing concern. Mr Lightfoot, who had the King's Head Hotel, built the brewery at Well Garth and Mr Theakston had the Black Bull in Silver Street with the brewery at the back. They both combined malt-roasting with brewing. In about 1870 Theakstons built a new brewery and malting in Red Lane.

Entries in the census who put themselves down as employing more than one worker are:

B. Ascough	Market Place	Tallow-chandler	2 men
J. Ascough	Market Place	Joiner	1 man 1 app.
G. Furby	Market Place	Shoemaker	1 man 1 app.
J. Lightfoot	Market Place	Inkeeper, brewer and maltster	8 men
W. London	Market Place	Tailor	6 men
M. Dresser (Mrs)	Park Street	Straw bonnet-maker	2 women
J. Ruecroft	Park Street	Woolcomber	4 men
H. Atkinson	Park Street	Tailor	2 apps.
W. Peniston	Red Lane	Basket maker	3 men
W. Jackson	Mill House	Miller	4 men
T. Stott	Market Place	Saddler	2 men
J. Cummings	Market Place	Woolcomber	11 men
T. Buckle	College Lane	Tailor	2 men
T. Pullen	College Lane	Coachbuilder	12 men
F. Sturdy	Silver Street	Shoemaker	2 men
M. Sturdy (Mrs)	Silver Street	Dressmaker	2 apps.
E. Jackson	Silver Street	Woolstapler	8 men

The following are the acreages of some of the farms and the number of men and women employed on them:

40 acres	1 man	33 acres	1 man
80 acres	2 men, 1 boy	162 acres	3 men
200 acres	3 men	214 acres	2 men
130 acres	2 men	170 acres	3 men, 2 boys 1 woman

Robert Theakston is not entered on the census as employing anyone; whether this was an omission or whether the fact that he had eight children meant this was truly a family business I am not sure.

From this and the list of occupations one can see that most people worked on their own or with one assistant or apprentice—in many cases this was their own son—at their own premises. There was also a travelling troop of actors visiting Masham at the time of the census.

Stone breakers on the road (*Costume of Yorkshire, 1814*)

There were some small industries in the villages. Ilton had a tannery and tile and brickworks as well as its lime kiln. The cotton mill at Healey has seven labourers entered in the census—two women and five men. The mines in Colsterdale were still a flourishing concern at the beginning of the century. In 1829 a new coal road was made from Gollingthye to Thorney Grane Colliery. Miners were paid 2s for a day's work and a corve (miner's basket) of coal was sold for 1s in 1820. There was even a mine in Arnagill but this was given up by Thomas Atkinson of Roundhill in 1825 as a losing concern. In 1856 Admiral Harcourt rented both the lead mines in Colsterdale and the coal mines as well.

A lot of the coal mined was of poorer quality and was used in the lime kilns to burn the limestone and produce lime which was used to improve the poorer land. There were quite a number of these kilns, one in Colsterdale, two at High Mains, one at Low Ellington, one at Sourmire and one at Ilton. There may have been other smaller ones but there is little trace of these.

Lime kiln in Colsterdale

As can be seen from the census below the population of the area was at its highest about the middle of the century. After this, industrialisation began to kill the smaller village industries and draw people to the factories.

	Fearby	Healey and Sutton	Swinton and Warthermarske	Masham
1801	205	354	174	1022
1811	216	354	182	1014
1821	214	413	177	1171
1831	249	400	207	1276
1841	237	*442*	*214*	*1318*
1851	*251**	378	205	1139
1861	242	317	202	1079
1871	216	270	171	1062
1881	222	244	152	1071
1891	228	209	176	1066
1901	187	184	174	995

* The numbers in italics show the decades when the population was at its highest in the various townships.

A dairy in the 1800s would consist of seven to ten cows. Seven cows would give enough milk to make two cheeses a day. Cheese was made in the summer and butter in the winter if there was any milk over. In the summer the cows were milked in the fields and the milk was carried back to the farm in backcans very often slung on either side of a donkey. In the 1840s at the cheese fairs at Leyburn the name Wensleydale was adopted for cheese made in this area. In 1890 the Department of Agriculture and Leeds University formed an advisory service with instructors on butter and cheesemaking to try and raise the standard—Lord Masham wrote to them suggesting that they might do better if they helped the farmers with selling their produce.

The following are some prices of animals in 1800:[4]

Sheep	17s
Oxen	£11 10s
Pigs	£2 12s

Rents were going up, and the following are examples of some of those paid by farmers on the moor edge in 1800:

Roundhill	£24
Grimesgill	£22
High Ashhead	£21
Arnagill	£20 (this was £14 in 1700 and £7 in 1600)

The milk boy (*Costume of Yorkshire, 1814*)

153

Farmers (*Costume of Yorkshire, 1814*)

The following are some of the estate expenses for the year 1830:[5]

Husbandry	£553	13s	8d
Housekeeping	£769	8s	
Gardens etc.	£458	19s	3d
Stables	£560	2s	10d
Servants	£337	15s	
Taxes etc.	£119	3s	4d
Annuities	£106	12s	4d
Building and repairs	£822	19s	8d
Other	£488	15s	2¼d

Income from the estate at the same time was:

Masham	£1518	16s	6d
Swinton	£554	4s	0d
Ilton cum Pott	£482	18s	6d
Fearby	£310	12s	6d
Healey	£1101	12s	6d
Ellingtons	£650	5s	0d
Ellingstring	£78	12s	6d
Colsterdale	£90	11s	6d

Summary of Tithe Schedule 1838

£163 rent to the Fellows and Scholars of Trinity College
£35 annual rent to the Rev. Waddington, Vicar of Masham

Township area: 2193 acres, 1 rood, 15 perches, excluding common land.
Land subject to tithe—the same

Arable land cultivated, subject to tithe	550 acres
Meadow land subject to tithe	1549 acres 1 rood 15 perches
Woodland	94 acres
Common land	6464 acres

Values 1838

Wheat	1 bushel	7s.	0¾d
Barley	1 bushel	3s.	11¼d
Oats	1 bushel	2s.	9d

In 1879 Mrs Danby-Harcourt died (the Admiral had died in 1863), and the estate went to Gilbert Affleck who took the name of Danby. However he decided to sell the estate and it was bought by Samuel Cunliffe-Lister, later the first Lord Masham. The story of his life shows how he brought a taste of the industrial revolution of these times to Masham.

Samuel Cunliffe-Lister was born at Calverley Hall near Bradford, the fourth son of an old landed family. They moved to the family seat at Manningham Hall near Bradford when Samuel was a small child and the most formative years of his life were thus spent in a region where the machine was beginning to grind out the first fascinating rumblings of the Industrial Revolution. Many possibilities of wealth and power were enticing men to invent what we now consider to be more primary machines. 'Invent' is perhaps the wrong word for such machines were really a mixture of inventions and developments and the country was so abuzz with new ideas and devices that perfectly honest men sometimes found themselves unwitting 'borrowers' of other men's ideas. Samuel Cunliffe-Lister first went to America to help his brother with his business in worsted manufacture and the shipping of goods to America. He crossed the Atlantic six times before he was 21 (this was in the days of sailing ships) and he looked back on his days in America as some of the very happiest of his life. He then came back and managed to persuade his reluctant father to finance the building of a power-driver combine and worsted spinning mill at Manningham. At 23 he was one of the proprietors and partners with a brother, who died shortly afterwards, and James Ambler. He then started to work on the development of a new woolcombing machine inspired by the somewhat primitive woolcombing machine invented half a century earlier by Dr Edmund Cartwright, inventor also of the power loom. The year before Lister had paid £12 000 to Donisthorpe of Leicester for patent rights. Now assisted by Donisthorpe he worked hard to develop a comb that could deal with the finer qualities of wool. Success came soon, and in less than a year he had orders for fifty machines and the distinction of being the first man to comb botany wool by power. A claim for infringement

Samuel Cunliffe-Lister

of patent rights were lodged against him in 1852 and the courts found that both parties had infringed each other's rights. Lister promptly paid £30 000 for the Heilmann comb rights (which he did not use), hurried on with his developments and was soon able to charge a royalty of £1000 on each machine incorporating his ideas. However he did not concentrate on machine-making but turned the whole of Manningham works over to woolcombing. In those days he could be seen regularly just before 6.0 am walking to the mill; his breakfast was brought to him by his son and daughter, and he would work till 7.30 at night with the rest of his employees.

When he was but little over forty Samuel Cunliffe-Lister had made himself successful and famous as the head of the world's woolcombing industry. He had in every way justified his 'descent into trade' and his triumph would have been enough—indeed too much for most men.

For him it was only the beginning. In 1855 he had seen a huge mass of unusable silk waste lying in a London warehouse and he could not put its challenge out of his mind. During the next decade he lost over £360 000, and yet another partner, experimenting with ways of utilising this unpromising mess of twigs, leaves, spoiled cocoons and dead silkworms. Yet it continued to be worthless as a textile raw material and could not even rank as manure, for it would not rot. Little wonder that the London silk 'throwsters' were glad to dump it on him at ½d a lb. But in 1865 he broke the riddle and put silk waste through a comb that in nine years bought and equipped two new mills. Whereupon he immediately reinsured by buying silk-growing estates in India. By 1867 commercial silk-spinning was quite successful and Lister merged his endeavours with Reizach in the even more fascinating problem of weaving silk velvet by power. Fire entirely destroyed the mills at Manningham in 1871 but he had saved his drawings, which was all he needed. He set about the building of the vast mills which remain that 27-acre heart of Manningham.

Over the years he took out 150 patents, ranging from a coal-cutting machine, an air brake for railway trains which he produced in 1848, a corn brick for use in wartime, as well as his more profitable ones in the wool trade. The *Dictionary of National Biography* credits him with the creation of the Australian wool trade.

He was a great benefactor to the town of Bradford and he sold Manningham Hall to the Corporation of Bradford in 1870 when he moved to Farfield Hall. They renamed it Lister Park in his honour and in 1875 they erected a statue of him. He was a great believer in Tariff Reform and with Lord William Bentinck founded the Fair Trade League. He spent a great deal of money on propaganda and wrote many pamphlets to explain his ideas.

Although he was 68 when he first came to Swinton he was far from retired and continued to work and write a great deal in support of Fair Trade as well as for the estate and his many other interests. He was granted a peerage in 1891 by Lord Salisbury, although he had previously refused one from Gladstone whom he bracketed with Peel as betrayers of English agriculture, and he took the title Lord Masham. He was a very good shot, and had a new pair of guns made for him at the

Samuel Cunliffe-Lister going shooting in his eighties

157

THE "CHEAP LOAF";

OR,

SOME FREE TRADE FALLACIES.

(As depicted by Mr. G. W. MEDLEY, at the Cobden Club Annual Meeting, 1890.)

BY

S. CUNLIFFE LISTER,

PRESIDENT OF THE NATIONAL FAIR-TRADE LEAGUE.

" Ah, John, the Squire and the rest of the neighbours are having French boots, and I have got nothing to do, and no money, and cannot buy your nice cheap foreign bread."—
(See page 7.)

PUBLISHED BY

THE NATIONAL FAIR-TRADE LEAGUE,

23, COCKSPUR STREET, LONDON, S.W.

1890.

(PRICE TWOPENCE.)

Cover of one of the many pamphlets written by Samuel Cunliffe-Lister to support the Fair Trade League and against Free Trade

age of 90! He was also a keen angler and was interested in coursing, keeping a good kennel of greyhounds at Swinton.

His coming to Swinton was viewed with some apprehension by the district as Mr P. C. Verity said: 'When the estate came into the hands of an owner who was a manufacturer it was thought that he would want to make money out of it, but he went round to see if the tenants were happy and comfortable. A dairy was built for the farmers because they were not getting the price they should for their produce, however it wasn't very successful as farmers did not understand business. They started to make cheddar cheese but it got dried and could not be sold, but "Mr Lister" stood the lot.'

Lord Masham's wife had died before he came to Swinton, leaving him with two sons and five daughters. Only one of his daughters married—the Rev. Charles Boynton and they had one daughter, the late Countess of Swinton. One of his sons also married but had no children. His eldest daughter kept house for him at Swinton. Mrs Bradford remembers how the children used to stand at the side of the road to watch her going to the Bedale Hunt Ball in her carriage with her footmen.

On 9 June 1875 the Masham–Melmerby railway line was opened. The opening day caused rejoicing in Masham and everyone who cared to go was transported to Ripon and back free of charge—in trucks of all sizes open and otherwise. The avenue of limes on the road entering Masham was planted by the Grammar school boys to commemorate the opening.

Masham Station in the 1880s

159

The fountain erected to commemorate
Queen Victoria's Golden Jubilee

In 1887 it was Queen Victoria's Golden Jubilee; she had been Queen for fifty years and there were celebrations all over the country to celebrate the occasion. In Masham money was raised to build a fountain to commemorate the day. On 23 June there was a celebration laying of the foundation stone with a procession from the Market Place. The following is a description from a press cutting:

The procession was headed by the Masham Volunteer Band, following these were the committee. They were followed by the horsemen, who were very much commented upon by the agricultural labourers and others in the district, almost every hamlet and village in the district being represented in the procession. Next in order were the children in waggons and children on foot, who cheered lustily as the procession moved along. These were followed by the order of 'Golden Fleece' whose peculiar attire was a great attraction, as were also the 'Millenary Sword Dancers' from Grewelthorpe. Then came the representative of the immortal 'Bishop Blaize' mitred and robed, and carrying his sceptre in his hand. The 'Shepherd and Shepherdess' came next, the latter of who was attired in a green dress, with a wand in her hand around which was entwined a quantity of hawthorn blossom and some of the same blossom also occupied a place around her hat. Next came the woolcombers, a class whose occupation is now almost if not altogether in the Masham district 'no more' carrying their formidable-looking 'combs' in their hands, their heads being covered with the old-fashioned paper caps. These persons, it may be remarked were men who formerly engaged in the work of woolcombing themselves and not the representatives of that class of people. The charcoal burner who occupied the back of the humble donkey had also a place in the procession, as well as the fire-engine, and other horsemen, and the rear was brought up by the Bedale string band. The procession proceeded towards Renton Well, where the foundation stone of the memorial fountain was laid by S. Cunliffe-Lister Esq., junior, in the presence of between 4000 and 5000 spectators. A platform had been erected at the site of the new fountain, which was decorated with flags, evergreens. After the opening ceremony and speeches the procession reformed and returned by Park-street to the Market Place where Bishop Blaize was presented with the usual address, and the sword dance was performed by the sword-dancers. Tea was then given to about 500 children and 800 adults in a large tent erected in the Market Place. The Bedale string band discoursed several choice selections of music at the Market Cross during the afternoon, and on the Holme during the evening, when dancing was indulged in. Several races were run on the Holme in the afternoon and evening, which were witnessed by a large number of people. Fire balloons were also sent up from the Market-place in the evening. The day was a thoroughly enjoyable one throughout and the church bells began to ring out joyously early in the morning and continued to peal at intervals during the day.

The procession of Bishop Blaize (*Costume of Yorkshire, 1814*)—this was once an annual event in Masham

Some of Swinton staff

From the list of subscribers to the memorial fund we can get an idea of the number of servants employed at Swinton at this time:

Mrs Scott	Dairy maid	J. Lawson
Inglis	F. Grange	H. Richardson
Shanebrook and family	1st footman	R. Heslop
Wray	2nd footman	E. Thorpe
Robinson	G. Dixon	W. Stanley
2nd housemaid	Swinton cowman	C. Richardson
3rd housemaid	Polisher	
4th housemaid	Roberts coachman	*Swinton keepers*
Head laundrymaid	Roberts groom	Coleman (head)
2nd laundry maid	Wagstaff helper	Graham
3rd laundry maid		Harvey
Kitchen maid	*Swinton gardeners*	Kay
Scullery maid	R. Agar (head)	George
Scaife	G. Backhouse	
White	A. Horner	
	W. Gill	

Swinton joiners, masons and labourers

Watson	Lockwood	Horner
Woodward Sen.	Kitching	Wharton
Woodward Jun.	Bradley	J. Rider
Mallaby	Prendergast	John Rider
J. Banks	G. Scaife	J. Walker
Youth Binks	C. Scaife	J. Metcalfe
James Binks	Coldbeck	G. Todd
Ellis	Atkinson	Mr Maister agent

These are the ones who subscribed; but there may have been others who did not. Witches and wise men were still feared and respected. In the 1800 list of field names we find two called 'witch's hole', one in Healey and another at Ellingstring. Mr Jack Reddington remembers his grandmother telling him how they had a cow calving and they were worried the witch was going to put a spell on it. They went to see the wise man in Masham who gave them a ball of something to put on the fire. They went home and locked all the doors and windows and did this. The old witch came and banged on the door and said she knew they had been to see the wise man—the calf was all right.

As can be seen from the number of dressmakers and shoemakers in the list of employments, everybody's clothes and shoes were still made to order. Dressmaking must have been a very useful way of earning some extra money for the women who were clever with their fingers. Clogs were worn by everybody on the farm until about the 1920s. In Masham these were made at Willow Garth and also at Birk Gill in Colsterdale where the clogmakers would put up their tents and use the available timber. Mrs Bradford remembers as a child playing truant from school and going down to Willow Garth and knocking down a great pile of clogs, for which she got into trouble.

The following odd subjects were some of the lectures given in the 1850s at the Mechanics Institute:

Mental Culture, Comparative Anatomy, Botany and Horticulture, Practical Phrenology, Agriculture, Wonders of the Dead Sea, Fairies of Early English Poetry, Witchcraft, Comets, Bells, Thunder Storms, a Night with the Chinese.

We get a picture of the literacy in Masham during this century from the numbers able to sign their name on the marriage register:

	Literate		*Illiterate*		*Total marriages*
1813	9 men	6 women	9 men	12 women	18
1832	14 men	11 women	3 men	6 women	17
1850	17 men	12 women	1 man	6 women	18
1875	15 men	14 women		1 woman	15

The old cell in Millgate

The Poor House was in Millgate with the old cell behind it. In 1885 this was being used as a powder warehouse, presumably by the Volunteers. These Volunteers, later to become the Territorials, were raised throughout the country in the 1850s because of ill-feeling against the British in France.

Mr Musgrave remembers his grandfather telling him of people being put in the cell so it must have been in use until about the middle of the nineteenth century.

13 **1900**

At the beginning of the century life in Masham was beginning to change but was still very different from what it is today. A number of the old traditions were still observed. The curfew bell was rung at 8 am and 5 pm. The old year was rung out and the new year rung in. On Shrove Tuesday the pancake bell was rung and the children were told that at 11 am pancakes were tossed over the church steeple. On the death of a Masham resident the death bell was rung. Alf Coldbeck, the church sexton, toured Masham ringing a bell to remind people of any event taking place on that particular day, as well as announcing any lost property. Riding the Stang still took place and one of the last culprits was Cocky Reynard who lived in the Market Place. Coronations and other festivals were always observed by the schoolchildren. Mrs Holland remembers dancing round the maypole at King George V and Queen Mary's coronation in 1911. There were also fancy dress parades.

School children maypole dancing at Healey at the beginning of the century

Wesleyan Chapel and Baptist chapel outing to Druids Temple in 1908

Celebrations at the coronation of King George V

Silver Street, Masham

Most of the transport consisted of horses and flat carts. Mrs Bradford remembers that when they lived in the Market Place it was her job as a child to take their horse down to a field behind Glebe House. Her father was a game dealer and used to take all the game from Swinton. This used to be brought down in the game cart driven by Robert Mallaby of Swinton Mill and John Glew of Burnholme. The game was packed into hampers and taken on their flat cart down to Masham station.

The roads were very bad and full of potholes. In winter it was particularly difficult to get around. Dr Cockcroft overcame this by having a sleigh with bells. These bells must have been a very welcome sound to anyone who was taken ill when the snow had brought other means of transport to a standstill. The children used to sledge down Millgate and in the field in front of Mill House. William Jackson who lived in Mill House used to get very cross with them for sliding on the hill and making it slippery.

Children always went out first-footing at Christmastime and the New Year, knocking on people's doors expecting sweets and fruit. At Barclay's Bank and Theakston's Brewery they were all given a penny. Sunday school treats in the summer were very much looked forward to. Farmers loaned hay carts and everyone sat on forms and sang songs *en route*. Tea was at one of the big farms or the Hackfall Inn which was very popular. Lord Masham and Miss Cunliffe-Lister gave a treat to the children of Masham and Ellington and Kell Bank schools on alternate years. The Masham children marched behind a band to Swinton where they were given quite valuable presents.

In 1906 at the age of 91, while he was on an election campaign with Joseph Chamberlain, Lord Masham caught pneumonia from which he died. He was succeeded by his eldest son Samuel Cunliffe-Lister.

The following are some extracts from a newspaper article written by James Duffield in 1938:

REMEDIES OF 100 YEARS AGO

INTERESTING RECORDS OF MASHAM'S OLD CHEMIST SHOP.

MEMORIES OF JOHN HAWKIN AND HIS MEDICAL HALL.

The chemist's shop in the Market Place, Masham, has a business record of more than 100 years. Could you have visited the town so long ago the sign of John Hawkin, Medical Hall, would have greeted you above the shop door.

There can be no doubt that John Hawkin was a progressive businessman for a glance into the remaining records of his trading account show that from this shop at Masham he supplied drugs and remedies throughout Wensleydale.

Much business was done in cattle medicines. A wrapper for cattle drinks dated 1840, gives a selection of testimonials from satisfied users. From Aysgarth, Wensleydale, Christopher Thompson adds his recommendation that others should try Hawkins Improved Horse Balsam. Mr George Barker, Pott Hall, near Masham, writes in 1844 that the composition for watering sheep improves the wool both in quantity and quality. From Preston, Wensleydale, Samuel Hammond expresses the opinion that the surest preventative for disease in young calves, is to use the drench obtainable only at the Masham address.

OLD-FASHIONED REMEDIES.

Hawkin's German Paste would remove grease without effort, and it was possible to purchase paste blacking, long life lozenges, essence for lameness, shepherds' tablets, bears' grease, black soap and the dales famous remedy, Dalby's Carminative.

John Hawkin was succeeded by Mr John Kendall, who unlike the previous owner, expended his energies on enterprises not wholly connected with shop interests. He provided the first water works for Masham.

On the site of the Marfield springs he made filter beds, erected pumping station and water tower, and by pipe line brought the supply to the town. The supply, though abundant, was exceptionally hard, and the undertaking was abandoned in favour of the present supply.

Rich in humour is the story of the resident who told the local doctor that he obtained almost all his medicine from his (the doctor's) understudy, the chemist. This was strongly denied, until it was pointed out that Kendall owned the water works. •

On the site of the police station, John Kendall had a garden and glass houses.

To look through the prescription book is to read pages of history. Here family medicines may be traced through generations up to the present and are still dispensed.

The shop contains many objects of interest. The large wooden bins were store places for linseed and dog biscuits. Lacquered stock tins, with quaint Chinese figures painted on the sides, made picturesque relics of the days when large stocks of tea and coffee were carried. The large iron pan was used to compound green ointment usually asked for as green salve.

STORED IN ATTICS.

In the attics may be found coffee grinding mills, a plant for filling shot gun cartridges, and in the corner stand a pair of wooden boot jacks. The large chest holds the music store of the old Masham Music Society, while on the wall shelves, closely resembling a museum, stand an assortment of ancient jars and galley pots.

On these premises there operates through each floor a winch and trap doors. In times past hundreds of bars of salt were stored to provide curing for farmhouse bacon.

One room resembles a miniature arsenal, in it is stored the equipment of the last Masham Volunteer Corps. There are rifles, bayonets, water bottles and trenching tools, and, until recently, the shop could boast sufficient drums and bugles to equip a bugle band.

You would not see all without a look at the kit of dental forceps for this was the dental clinic too. When the kit was spread along the rear counter it was enough to strike fear into the heart of the bravest Dalesman. The apprentice had the task of holding the patient's wrists while dental extraction was performed in skilled manner without an anæsthetic.

PEDLARS' PURCHASES.

Pedlars call even to-day to purchase a supply of lavender and naphthalene balls before tramping the dales.

Mr Powley, Mr J. Wade, and its present owner, Mr Plumber, complete the list of men who have preserved the familiar atmosphere of the shop throughout the years.

Very different is the display of merchandise now offered for sale but here and there an old favourite may still be noticed waiting for the customer who thinks that even in modern pharmacy there is nothing quite so good.

As you leave the shop the worn stone floor slabs seem to echo the words of Shakespeare: 'Faithfully ministering to relieve the many ills which flesh is heir to'.

Market Place, Masham

Bowling
Green

Pavilion

·361

7·535
Recreation Ground

MASHAM

14·415

N
↑

U . . . r

a . . . e . . . r

F.P.

F.P.

F.P.

247
·857

Mi

F. P.

rammar School

Nutwith House

3

242°
·825

B. M. 282·1

280 +

MILLGATE

Vicarage

St. Mary's Church
(Vicarage)

'S. D   2·648
Grave Yard

F.P.

F.P.

4·407

1·981

51

Glebelands

274

1. Private school
2. Saddler's shop (Burtons of Ripon)
3. Beckwith's boot repair shop where nails etc. could be bought
4. Todd's—tailor
5. Mr Atkinson—vet
6. Dr Williams
7. Sweet shop—Mr Walker
8. Grocer—Mr T. Verity
9. Drapers—Mr Tenant
10. Mechanics Institute
11. Blacksmith's shop—Mr Atkinson
12. The muffin shop—Mrs Wintersgill
13. Ironmonger—Mr Jefferson
14. Butcher—Mr W. Gill
15. Dr A. Brown
16. Gentleman's Club
17. Millers—I'Ansons
18. Coach builders
19. Mrs Reynard's tea shop
20. Midland Bank
21. Draper—Mr W. Carter
22. Fishing tackle—Mr Todd, Hatmaker—Mrs Todd
23. Dressmaker—Mrs Jackson, Photographer—Mr Jackson
24. Wool shop—Mr C. F. Bruce
25. Posting house—Ryders
26. Barclay's Bank
27. Builder—Mr Akers (he was also a well-known preacher)
28. Dr Cockcroft
29. Grocer—Mr Gill
30. Butcher's shop—Mr Ackroyd
31. King's Head—Mr Harper
32. Grocer—Mr Pickersgill
33. Wesleyan Manse
34. Vicarage
35. Edmondson & Gowland Solicitors
36. Dressmaker—Mrs Mudd
37. Tailor—Mr Leathley
38. Chemist—Mrs Powley
39. Ironmonger—Mr Clarke
40. Post Office—Mr Mood (later first caretaker to new Town Hall)
41. Butcher's Shop—Mr Lambough
42. Police Station
43. Bruce Arms—Mr Wilson
44. Painter and decorator—Mr Finlayson
45. Bay Horse—Mr Broadley
46. Draper and shoes—Mr Metcalfe
47. Butcher—Mr Wintersgill
48. Saddler—Mr Patrick
49. Grocer—Peacocks
50. Tailor—Mr Buckle
51. Greengrocers—Miss Elsworth

52. Mr Fishpool—monumental mason
53. Joiner—Mr Bill Thwaites
54. Primitive Chapel
55. Coal merchant—Mr J. Hill
56. Boot repairs—Mr Bennison
57. Shoes and undertaker—Mr G. Towler
58. Cobbler—Mr T. Sturdy
59. White Bear—Mr Lambert
60. Guest House, Mrs Auton
61. Tailor—Mr Carter
62. Brewery—Mr Theakston
63. Cobbler—Mr A. Duffield
64. Brewery—Mr Lightfoot
65. Guest House—Mrs Wilkinson
66. Rowantree's Cheese Factory
67. Shoe repairer

Blacksmith in College Lane

Barrel organ in Church Street, Masham

173

Silver Street, Masham

As can be seen from the map of Masham in 1908 there were a great many more shops then there are now. Running these entailed a lot of hard work for some of their owners. Mrs Sparkes remembers her mother running a tea shop—she did all her own baking and during Masham Fair time she would be up all night. She could seat 20 to 25 people and charged 2s 6d (12½p) for a three to four-course dinner. She lived there until she died at over 90.

There were still a number of shops and small businesses in the villages. There was a general store and blacksmith in Ilton. Fearby had two inns, two general stores, a

The Black Horse pub, Healey

174

Opening of the Town Hall

grocer, a butcher and a blacksmith. Healey had a Post Office, one inn, a blacksmith and a cornmill. Ellingstring had a blacksmith, a general store and an inn.

The first Lord Masham left £5000 for the benefit of Masham. The second Lord Masham formed a trust of Masham people to decide how the money could be put to best use. It was decided that £1700 should be spent on building an isolation hospital at Marfield and that the rest should be spent on building a Town Hall incorporating the Mechanics Institute which was proving too small. The new Town Hall was opened by the second Lord Masham on 31 May 1913.

The second Lord Masham opening the Town Hall in 1913

175

Masham sheep fairs

Up until the First World War the sheep fairs were still great events in Masham. Mrs Prentice at Ilton remembers watching the droves of sheep coming over from Nidderdale with the farmers on ponies. They were kept in fields around Masham until the fair day. I think the following newspaper article tells us what the fairs meant to those who lived in Masham.

MASHAM FAIRS

A Child's Recollection

(From a Correspondent)

Christmas excepted, there is no memory of my childhood so clear to me as that of the 'fairs.' To no other part of the year, except again to Christmas, did we children—it is more than forty years ago—look forward with such excited anticipation of delight. The very things that heralded it were all so pleasant—red apples in the orchards, the golden hue of harvest, the acrid smell of garden bonfires, the first touch of frost in the evening air betokening the 'back end.'

September 17th was the date in our calendar thus redly marked; and the day before the little town used to be aclash with the heavy wedges driving in the hurdles for the pens. There were pens covering the market-place and pens along the street and even pens—to our great rejoicing—in front of our house. I have often wondered since if my mother, sitting at her sewing behind the brown wire blinds of the dining-room, disliked the smell of sheep; but seeing she made no complaint, I take it that the fairs without it—even for her—would not have been the fairs. And what a thrill it was to be wakened before dawn by the coming of the sheep. The patter of their little feet along the dusty road past our house was just like rain. A mighty host they were in those days, flock after flock—staid black-faced Southdowns, Cheviots with queer blotches on their brown faces and

176

scared eyes, little horned Scotch sheep with fleeces almost as long as petticoats were in those days, and in spite of them as agile at leaping over a stone wall or a stack-bar as any two-year-old. And what a tumult there was of mingled sound—here the shrill bleating of some frightened ewe, there the raucous reassurance of some old ram, with little lamblike voices in between, pathetic as all little voices are; and dominating them all the sharp yelp of a watchful sheep-dog heading back some would-be truant.

Three days the fairs lasted; and the sheep fair on the first day was certainly the busiest. The tiny town seethed with dogs and men, ewes and lambs. Wiry lean sunburnt men from the dales, a curious spring in their walk come of much walking over heather; stout, prosperous farmers from the richer lowlands, with so much more in their pigskin purses that the taut ring about the middle was like a fashionable waist; not to mention all the worthies—Masham 'standards'—of the town. Of them I could name everyone but will not, seeing how since then the churchyard sod has covered most of those whom in, my simplicity I though so important as to be immortal. There were shepherds too, in long coats and fustian trousers and with strangely quiet faces as if their winter watching in the fold at lambing-time gave them a more thoughtful cast then those of other men; and Irish drovers, excitable and getting drunk long before an Englishman on the same amount of liquor would have turned a hair. Stick in hand—for no child was ever without a stick at fairtime though I am afraid its main purpose was to prod some woolly, throbbing back—we children would wedge our way through the crowd about some pen and, mimicking the talk about us, would bandy with one another such cryptic phrases (for us then) as hogs and wethers, gimmers and shearlings.

On the second day horses and cattle were sold, and though we were not allowed too near the latter we found excitement enough in watching the horses being trotted up and down the street and the haggling that took place. Bargaining in those days was solemn and took time, and had a curious ceremonial that did we copy it in our childish play was not always sanctioned by our elders. Do they still clap hands and spit, I wonder, as they did when I was a child? Or has the spitting and clapping disappeared as they tell me the fairs themselves have disappeared until nowadays they are little more than a name?

But the third day was *the* day. By midday sheep, cattle, and horses had gone; and in the market-place the pens had been taken down and stalls set up, where old women with black hair and gilt earrings sold sweets and fairings; and round the Cross were swings and a gaily coloured Merry-go-Round. All three fair days to keep open house was the custom; and in every dining-room of consequence were spread great rounds of beef and legs of mutton, red pickled cabbage, damson pies and cream for any friend who chose to come. Now on the third fair day masters and servants, hosts and guests, children and sweethearts, farmlads and farm lassies crowded about the stalls. Fairings were bought and exchanged—shell boxes with a Present From Masham on their velvet covers, china mugs and jugs and plates with the same inscription, ribbons and lace, jewellery and rings; and many a dilatory courtship resolved itself into a solemn pledge at the stall where rings were sold. If it were a warm day wasps flew in swarms about the booths and clustered on the gingerbread and toffee.

For we, who were children, it was the happiest day of all the year. Such unaccustomed largesse of silver coins filled our little pockets, such reckless schemes of expenditure on sweets and cocoanuts agitated our little minds. Swings and those cruder side shows—Fat Women and the like—were forbidden; but upon the hobby horse we could ride as long as our means and stomach permitted.

25 lb Salmon caught by Mr W. Moon in September 1932 just above Masham Bridge

Hounds meeting at the White Bear Hotel

There were no gilded swans then or fairy chariots or monstrous grotesque figures as there are now; but what a glorious cavalcade they were those wooden horses, black, roan and dappled grey, with their manes and tails of genuine horse hair and such spirit in their arched necks and glowing eyes and distended nostrils as would not have disgraced the swiftest Arab stallion of the plains.

Somehow those horses and the grinding music that accompanied them have remained in my memory clearest of all; for when, our money spent, we had gone home and had our suppers and been put to bed, we could still hear the hurdy-gurdy and the whistle that was the signal for yet another breathless ride. And so, with that strident whistle striking athwart our dreams, away we galloped on our fiery horses, black, roan and dapple grey, into the soundless realms of happy sleep.

The Yore was still a salmon river at the beginning of the century as can be seen in the photograph opposite. Hunting was also popular in the district. Lady Masham kept the Bedale hounds at Swinton at the beginning of the 1920s and Major Burrill started up the West of Yore pack about 1925 and kept the hounds at his home, The Greens.

The first major change to come to the district was the making of the Roundhill reservoir in 1901, and the building of the narrow gauge railway from Masham up to Fairthorn for the transport of the men and materials. A camp of wooden huts was built at Fairthorn to house the men who lived there for five years.while the reservoir was being built.

At first the railway was only built from Leighton to Fairthorn. Materials were brought up from Masham to Leighton by the haulage contractor Arthur Atkinson with his two steam traction engines, 'Majestic', and another said to have recently returned from service in the South African war. However this broke up the roads and after complaints Harrogate extended the railway to Masham.

It was opened in 1906 and in 1910 the railway was sold to Leeds corporation for their Leighton reservoir works. Leeds built an extension of the railway across the road to the camp at Breary Banks and then up to Spruce Gill Beck. This was probably when they still planned to build the reservoir in Colsterdale—this was

The building of the narrow gauge railway in the field at Low Burton

179

The camp at Fairthorn

The building of the dam at Roundhill reservoir

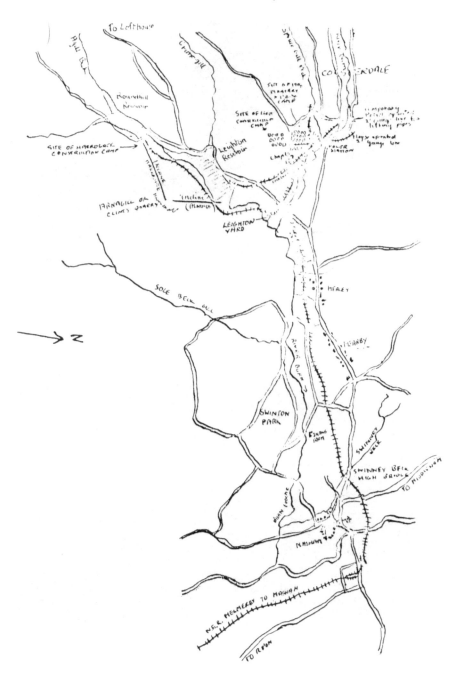

Map showing the route of the narrow gauge railway

Healey Mill

The Leeds Pals Battalion being dismissed on its arrival in camp

abandoned in 1907 owing to difficulties of strata, and they had to pipe the water to Leighton where they made a holding reservoir.

The Breary Banks camp consisted of 50 wooden buildings, including a hospital mission, recreation rooms and married quarters. Work on the reservoir started in 1908 but was interrupted by the First World War when the camp was taken over by the Leeds Pals. Mr Arthur Wynn, one of the Leeds Pals who first went to Breary Banks, wrote the following memories of those days:

On a sunny day in September 1914 the engine driver shut off the steam as we approached Masham Station and the engine and coaches ran gently into the station, as the train stopped carriage doors were flung open and out poured nearly 1000 men of the newly formed 'Leeds Pals Battalion'.

We were quickly formed into companies and with our kit bags on our shoulders we started our march to Colsterdale. The Commanding Officer rode his horse at the head of the Battalion. We marched across the bridge that spans the river Ure then along the avenue to climb the White Bear Bank, where Masham folk were gathered to watch us march past. We marched out of Masham up the Fearby Road heading West towards the camp with about five miles of mostly uphill marching. We passed through Fearby—a long rambling village of cottages and farmhouses—and then Healey. On the right just out of this village a Mr Gregg, the miller, was stood in front of the mill watching us march past; it was at this mill that corn was ground for the local farmers. Another half mile and we were in view of the camp. We now had to climb two very steep banks known as Breary Banks. The camp consisted of three rows of tents and three rows of navvies huts, now empty, but which had been used by men working on the Leeds Reservoir. There were about ten in our tent and we slept with our feet towards the pole. As far as I can remember 'roll call' was at 9.0 p.m. and at 9.30 the bugler blew 'Light's Out' and at 10 p.m. he blew the 'Last Post'; what mournful notes they were on our first night at Breary Banks.

The light railway brought up most of the foodstuffs etc. from Masham Station; this narrow gauge railway ran right into the camp. The little steam engine was powerful enough to pull three or four long open waggons loaded with foodstuffs for the 1000 or so officers and men at Colsterdale, but the engine was very wide in proportion to the narrow gauge lines, this made it sort of top heavy and quite often it would run off the lines. When a batch of Leeds Pals had been on leave, Tom Legg the engine driver would pack us into the long waggons. When we passed over the wooden bridges spanning the Ure and the Burn I always got ready to jump in case the engine ran off the line and into the stream below.

Luckily it was not many weeks before more wooden huts had been erected and we were able to move out of the tents as we were beginning to feel the cold nights of October. Most of my time at Colsterdale centred on the Motor Transport Section of the Leeds Pals when I drove a 2 ton Karrier wagon 'the old Belsize'. We were loaned a number of cars namely: a model T Ford, an open-tourer Sunbeam, and open-tourer Daimler and an open-tourer Vauxhall. In the early days at Colsterdale we were supplied with petrol etc by a Mr Tom Calvert who had a garage in Masham. He was a trained engineer who had served his time with one of the ship-building firms in the North East. I remember he was building a two-seater small car, it had wire wheels with a two cylinder water-cooled engine already in the chassis, but he was awaiting a gear box from the manufacturers. Alas with war work they were unable to supply and the project had to be dropped.

One Sunday Mr Calvert invited me to his home at 'Sunnyside' where the little river 'Swinney' runs through the garden. At lunch that day Mr Calvert's mother was sat at the head of the table, she was dressed all in black with a white lace head covering, she reminded me of the late Queen Victoria.

Mr Percy Wharton, a blacksmith in College Lane gave us free use of his shop for doing repairs. Almost immediately across the road from this was an ivy-covered cottage with a small shop adjoining; here lived a Mr and Mrs Musgrave and their daughter. Mrs Musgrave used to bake lovely loaves of white bread and also sold sweets in the little shop. Mr Musgrave was in partnership with a Mr Thackwray as coach builders.

At camp it was getting towards the bad weather and the door most used by the 30 men in our hut was quite often damp with our chaps passing in and out and the wind drove in relentlessly; later when the snow started round the door there was often a pool of water. It was near the door that our senior NCO, Corporal Hare, put down his ground sheet and blankets, he had picked the worst place in the hut when he could have had the best, so much for the spirit of the Leeds Pals. When the battalion arrived in France a shell burst in the trench and Corporal Hare received almost the full blast in his face, he was disfigured for life, but by God's good grace his eyesight was saved.

The camp was later used as a German prison-of-war camp. The rest of the district was also affected by the war. A great many volunteers joined up and went to war, some never to be heard of again. Those who stayed also played their part in the war effort. Lady Masham, wife of the third Lord Masham who had succeeded his

Nurses and soldiers outside the Town Hall

brother in 1917, ran the Town Hall as a convalescent home for soldiers from Leeds and many of the young ladies of Masham helped in the kitchen and with the general running. There was also an infantry training camp on Roomer Common.

The following extracts from the parish magazine tell us something of those who went to war:

February 1916
The War has been brought very near to us in the death on the battle-field of two young heroes connected with this parish. The first to give his life for his country was Pte Walter Dodd, of the Northumberland Fusiliers, son of the late Mr John Dodd, for some years resident at Leighton Bridge, who worthily filled the important office of Sidesman of Healey Parish Church.

And in the middle of January the whole parish was shocked to hear that a similar sacrifice had been made by Rifleman Alfred Monkhouse, King's Royal Rifles, son of Mr Monkhouse, of Roundhill in this parish. He died gloriously whilst bandaging a wounded comrade in the trenches, and his death is deplored by all. A touching and very largely attended Memorial Service in his memory was conducted by the Vicar at Moorheads Service Room on January 16th.

March 1916
The Vicar has recently received an interesting letter from Captain Neil of the Leeds 'Pals' Battalion, who are now in Egypt. The following extract is especially gratifying: 'Two Fearby boys, Gill and Jackson, are in my Company, and it may interest you to know that these two men are amongst the best soldiers of my Company. They are excellent fellows, ready to endure hardships; reliable at all times, and they have the advantage over the men that have come from the towns, because they are not afraid of hard manual work'.

August 1916
The terrible fighting that is going on in France is taking its toll among our dear ones. Lance-corporal Nottingham (who has so long escaped in the severest fighting), Harry Gill and Slater Harrison are wounded. While great anxiety is felt for Fred Jackson, who at the time of writing had not been heard of since the beginning of July. Marvellous have been the escapes from certain death even among those who are the subjects of our daily intercessions. To take only two or three instances which have come under the Vicar's notice. One of our young heroes owes his life to his water-bottle, which was pierced by shrapnel, another had his pocket book pierced, while over the head of another a shell exploded, and the fragments were scattered all around him while he himself was unharmed.

At the end of the war a trust was formed to make a recreation ground in Masham in memory of those in Masham who had died during the war. Lord Masham offered them either the field on the riverside or the field on the King's Head farm where the tennis courts and cricket pitch then were. It was decided by one vote to accept the riverside field. A cricket club and a bowling club was formed and the field was fenced and let for sheep grazing. Lord Masham arranged for ash to be sent from the mills at Manningham by train to Masham to lay the foundations for the bowling green. The cricket pitch was then also laid out.

With the war over work on Leighton reservoir was continued and finished in 1924. Other changes came gradually; in 1914 two Bradford men leased the Masham mill premises from Lord Masham and formed the Masham Electricity

Corporation. They later sold the corporation to the Masham UDC who in turn sold it to the Cleveland and Durham Electricity Company in 1929. This brought an end to the tallow candles and paraffin lamps and the beginning of an easier way of life. It was 1938 however before electricity was taken to the villages outside Masham and a further 35 years before it reached all the more inaccessible farms in the district.

In 1929 during a reorganisation of local government it was proposed that Masham UDC should be joined with Bedale or Leyburn. This was strenuously opposed by the Masham councillors who pointed out that in Masham they had:

a first-class water supply;
two fire engines, steam and manual and a voluntary fire brigade;
a very good hospital;
their own gas works;
their own electricity concern.

It was eventually decided that Masham should remain on its own and in 1934 it was changed from an urban to a rural district.

Plumbing was also beginning to be modernised. Earth closets were being replaced by WCs and in 1935 the RDC made it compulsory for these to be fitted. At the beginning of the century water was still coming from pumps in the street—there was one in Morton Row—and the best water in the district came from the spring at Dixon Keld.

In the country areas it was many years before most of the houses got running water. Mrs Prentice of Ilton remembers having to carry water from the well to her house in buckets right up to the 1950s. At first she got it from a well by the Masham road; however she used to find the water rather stirred up when she went in the

Earth closet

Pump at Low Mains

186

morning and at first thought this was because of the farmer at Manor Farm drawing water for his pigs. She decided to get up at 6.0 am to get there before he did, but this made no difference and one morning when she lifted the lid she found some enormous rats in it. The council then stopped them using this well and she had to go to another at the top of Ilton; but this still meant getting up at 6.0 am to get her water before the cattle drank from it.

But in 1935 the houses in Morton Row as well as Cross Hills were demolished as being unfit for human habitation. Dixon Keld was also filled in as it was found too difficult to keep it in a reasonable state. It was then that the first twelve council houses were built in Marfield Lane at a cost of £4200 to house those who had lived in the demolished houses.

With the increase in more car ownership coming petrol pumps were being installed and the roads were also being improved, and by 1930 many of them had been tar-sprayed; 1931 saw the end of passenger services on the railway. Services had always been light and it was probably the traffic brought by the building of the reservoir which had prolonged the service until then.

At the beginning of the century life at Swinton was still lived in much the same way as it had been during the previous hundred years with about twenty servants in the house consisting of:

Butler, under-butler, usher of the hall, footman, housekeeper, 5 housemaids, ladiesmaid, 2 still-maids (they baked the bread), cook, 3 kitchenmaids, 3 laundry maids.

Mr Barlow remembers going to Swinton as an usher of the hall in 1919 for £24 a year. The third Lord and Lady Masham did quite a lot of entertaining and Mr Jack Musgrave remembers going up with others from Masham to provide the music at some of these parties. Lady Masham was a keen huntswoman and was master of the Bedale hounds which were kept at Swinton.

Apart from having installed their own electricity plant at the beginning of the century conditions on the estate were changing very little. In 1910 thirty-four people were employed:

3 masons	4 labourers
4 carpenters	3 carters
2 blacksmiths	2 slaters
2 sawyers	6 gardeners
8 woodmen	

In 1924 this had fallen to twenty-eight but in 1930 it had risen again to fifty-one which must have helped with the terrible unemployment of this period. In 1932 it was suggested that a recreation room should be built for the use of the unemployed. However Lady Swinton (then Lady Cunliffe-Lister) suggested that the money would be better spent in giving employment to as many people as possible and this could be done in improving the recreation gound and turning the field opposite the Post

Swinton staff

Office into a park and approach to the recreation ground. This plan was un-
animously agreed on by the Trustees and Lady Swinton let the field to them for one
shilling a year, money was raised and the work was carried out.

Wages were steadily rising as can be seen from the figures of a mason's wages:

1910 £1 7s
1918 £1 17s
1924 £2 5s
1931 £2 10s

Farm rents were also rising as shown by Manor Farm, Fearby rents below (per
annum):

1910 £144 10s
1915 £164
1927 £192

Lord Masham first bought a car about 1910. Mr Harold Ward remembers Mr
Beale the chauffer telling him how he had driven the carriage and horses until Lord
Masham had decided to buy a Daimler car when he (Mr Beale) had been sent to
Daimlers to learn how to drive it. In 1926 a lorry was bought for driving the guns
out shooting but most of the estate transport continued to be horsedrawn. The

keepers' trap which was made in Masham by Mr Musgrave now belongs to Dr Anderton. On shooting days the beaters from Masham had to walk up to the moors before they even started beating and it was not until after the Second World War that all the estate transport became mechanised.

In 1924 on the death of her uncle, Lady Swinton (then Lady Lloyd-Graeme) had inherited the Swinton estates and she and her husband, Sir Philip Lloyd-Graeme changed their name to Cunliffe-Lister. The lords of Mashamshire were once again involved in national politics. For nine years apart from brief interruptions caused by two Labour governments Sir Philip Cunliffe-Lister was President of the Board of Trade dealing with the many difficult problems of this post-war decade. In 1931 he was made Colonial Secretary and was created Viscount Swinton. In 1934 Mashamshire joined Lord and Lady Swinton and their family in the celebrations on the coming of age of their eldest son Mr John Cunliffe-Lister. There were celebrations again two years later at his wedding.

These celebrations must have been welcome breaks in the hard times of these years. Farmers had to work long, hard hours for very small return. Rowantree's had a dairy in Masham and paid farmers 5d (approx 2p) a gallon for their milk. In 1925 the farmers decided to form their own dairy to try and get a bit more for their milk. They bought some premises at Wellgarth and established a manufacturing dairy. Taking milk down to Masham by horse and cart meant long hours on the farms. Mrs Prentice remembers cutting the hay with horses and having to start at 4.0 am. Sheep were still washed before they were clipped and there were many sheep washes in the district. One of the most used was the one above the bridge at the golf course.

Lord and Lady Swinton with their sons John and Philip Cunliffe-Lister

Mr Tom Pearson who used to farm Quarry Gill Farm tells us of some of his memories of farming in the years before the First World War and the coming of tractors:

Learning to control a horse plough is something similar to driving a car for the first time. It just seems to have a will of its own and goes anywhere but where you want it to. I soon learnt that it was unwise to walk too much within the plough stilts or handles. If you did so you were asking for a nasty crack in the ribs if the plough sock or share should strike a stone when you were going along. Horses are very intelligent animals and wonderful company to share a job like ploughing. When you had ploughed to the end of the furrow you could let your horses have a wind, they would usually eat the grass in the hedge bottom whilst you sat on the plough stilts and had a rest as well. You did not need a watch to tell you when it was dinner time, working horses could do this for you. As it got nearer to going home time the pace would slow down and on reaching the headland they would attempt to turn for home. After ploughing came harrowing. This was a job that did not call for quite the same amount of skill as ploughing but it was not long before you learned not to follow directly behind. This was dangerous because should one of the harrows catch a big stone it would stop dead in its track, the other would shoot forward and before you knew where you were you would have your feet mixed up in them. Drilling corn with horses was a job that called for skilful control of horses and drill by the horseman. The method of yoking the horses to the drill was rather different, enabling the horseman to walk either left or right of the corn drill so he could see the mark left by his drill in the last run. The grass cutter and self-binder was also yoked up in the same way. Cutting corn with the self-binder was one of the most interesting

Ploughing with horses

190

of all the jobs that we did with horses. What with driving the horses and adjusting all the various levers and handles you were kept busy. The knife bar had to be kept just above the ground, clear of stones but not too high or you would leave stubble that was too long. The packers and knotter were also adjustable forward and backward to cater for crops of various lengths.

Whenever the thresher (which was then both pulled about and driven by steam) came into the district it was an event of great stir and importance. Literally everybody was involved in some way or other. A threshing day demanded a good staff of usually twelve to fourteen hard-working men. To get these men the local farmers employed a system of exchange. I often got the job of going round the neighbouring farms on a bike after milking and asking for one or two men to come to help out. I would continue round until sufficient men had been gathered up to make our day possible. As the thresher went from farm to farm it was our job to return the labour that we had borrowed. As the thresher got nearer to Quarry House a whole lot of preparatory work had to be done—the corn granaries had to be tidied, rat holes filled up, leaking roofs mended, sacks sorted and mended. We also had to provide and get ready coal for the steam engine which needed five to seven hundredweight per day. In the house mother would be baking extra bread, scones, tea cakes and fruit pies, cleaning and peeling potatoes, scraping carrots, steeping peas, preparing cabbages etc. all in readiness for the next day's threshing dinner at midday when all the helpers would come into the house and sit down to a splendid hot meal. The meals in this district were reckoned to be some of the best by the men in charge of the steam engine. The men would come and park the engine the night before and be back at 6.30 am to rake out the clinkers and brighten up the fire, leaving the engine to get up steam while they had breakfast and we did the milking. It was dusty and noisy work. Two men would fork up the sheaves, one would cut the bands and hand the sheaves to the feeder, others would carry away the battens of straw coming from the machine and the full sack of corn putting empty ones in their place. The man in charge of the engine would be busy keeping a good fire going while someone else would take the horse and cart to the nearest beck to fill up empty milk churns with water to keep the engine filled up so it didn't run out of steam.

Before we put in our own milking machine and lighting plant everything was to do by hand. We had to carry bucket, stool and a paraffin lantern from one cow byre to another in winter months. I learned to milk by hand at the age of six and was able to milk a cow which was in full milk dry in a few minutes. At eight years old I was milking two and three every morning before I got ready to walk to school and then again in the evening after I had come home. It was a great day when Father put in a milking machine in 1946. I persuaded him to buy an engine that was air-cooled in preference to water cooled and I hoped to get it to drive a generator for electric lighting as well as the vacuum pump for the milking machine. I got a dynamo from a scrap motor car, put it on to a metal base and drove it with a vee-belt from the engine. At first I got a single light into each cow byre using car headlamps at various points which was a vast improvement on the paraffin lanterns. Gradually I added more lights and eventually wired up the house, got a larger ex-RAF generator, and it was a very important day in October 1946 when we lifted the main switch and lit the whole house up for the very first time with electricity. It was only twelve volts but the light that it gave was far superior to any paraffin lamp.

Children on the Market Cross at the beginning of the century

Children going to school would have to walk quite a long way if they lived on outlying farms. There were many more schools in the district than there are now and children would stay at them throughout their school life. As well as the Grammar and Free schools in Masham there were also schools in the following villages:

Ilton (closed 1940s)
Fearby and Healey—Kell Bank
Colsterdale (closed 1920s)
Moorheads (closed 1920s)
Ellingstring (closed 1950s)

The following are extracts from parish magazines:

December 1918
Gratifying reports have been received from the Diocesan Inspector as a result of his recent visi₁ to the four Day Schools of the Parish. We give them in full:

Healey. Very good work is being done in this school. The answering throughout was intelligent, while the composition [on an old Testament subject] of the highest group was clear and concise. The repetition of the infants is by far the best in this district of 73 schools.

Ellingstring. The children of both divisions answered well, and their answers grasped the meaning of their lessons. Their written work was good.

Moorheads. An excellent tone prevails in this school, and the results of the examination reflect great credit on the mistress.

Ilton. A very comprehensive syllabus was offered by this school, and the children displayed a good knowledge of bible subjects and of the early part of the catechism. The hymn was sung with correctness and expression and the repetition was accurate, but it would sound better if taken more slowly and quietly.

The following entries from the Healey School Log Book give us an idea of the schooling of the earlier part of the century:

1900

May 11 The average attendance is only 46.4. The girls have attended badly. The excuse is 'Staying at home to help mother with spring cleaning'.

August 31 The attendance for the week is only 37. Harvesting is interfering with the attendance, several boys being away 'band making'.

December 13 Attendance has suffered this week through storms and bad weather.

April 30 Mr Snowden, Temperance Lecturer took the science lesson this morning on 'Alcohol and its effects'.

June 21 Admitted ... Kelvington, aged 7 years 2 months. He has not previously attended any school.

September 22 Only 43 in the afternoon, owing partly to Messers. Bostocks and Womburell's Menagerie at Masham.

November 1 In the afternoon as Eva Jackson was troublesome I sent her home, and her sister Constance saying 'Have I to go and all' I said 'Yes'. The girl Constance is also troublesome.

October 23 The exercise books for the lower classes have not yet arrived and in consequence most of the work is being done on slates.

The schoolhouse at Ellingstring

193

Mr Tom Pearson also remembers going to school:

In our early school days my sister Mary and I used to attend Ilton school. To get to school we had a walk of almost one and a half miles across our own land, the land of Hill Top farm and then along a narrow lane through some of the High Field farmland. During some of the heavy snowfalls that we got in the winter months our walks to and from Ilton school were often cold, wet and miserable. Mother used to wrap us up well in good thick clothing and we always wore wellingtons and carried our newly cleaned shoes in a separate bag. Mary would carry our shoes and I would carry our dinners which mother had packed for us complete with a bottle of milk. We quite frequently arrived at school with no milk having dropped it out of our dinner bag whilst opening a difficult gate or climbing a fence. When we got a really heavy fall of snow we used to go to school on our horse's back. That mare knew that she had us to take and seemed to enjoy it. Father would get her out of the stable, put on a bridle and short reins with a good thick layer of sacking as a saddle and up we would get. Next would come the dinner bag and shoe bag and then off we would go. Father would go with us and open the gates and leave them open as nearly all the stock would be inside on winter keep. We would ride Darling as far as Hill Top farm buildings and then get off her back, turn her round, give her some cow cake and a pat and set her off home.

The last of the thatched cottages were disappearing. The ones at Swinton were modernised in 1930. Willie Lambert, who was well known in the district for his poetry wrote the following poem about the thatched cottage on Roomer Common:

Thatched houses at Swinton

194

Thatched cottage on Roomer

The Old Thatched Cottage on the Moor

Out on the lonely moors you can see a cottage stand,
It is an ancient cottage, and yet it's sweet and grand,
It has an old thatched roof, and it's just a storey high,
Bonnie little cottage, you're a picture to my eye.

You're on the lonely moorland, far from the city crowd,
The blackbird and the robin they sing to you aloud.
The whinbush and the bracken grow just beyond the gate;
You may be small and humble, but I think you are great.

In that cottage lived a lady, and she was sweet and kind,
In every sense a lady, an example to mankind,
For ninety years she smiled as she trod Life's Great Highway;
But now she has departed to where the angels stay.

I see the golden sunset, the sky around is red,
The darkening night is dreary, and clouds roll overhead,
Yes, you have been shelter to many from the storm;
And for the family circle, you've been a place called home.

'Tis true the human race must have some place in which to dwell,
This country calls for houses, so build and build them well,
Old cottage, down the ages, you gave mankind your best,
Sweet flowers in the garden, and music, peace and rest.

And now, my old thatched cottage, to you I say farewell,
No more people under your old thatched roof shall dwell,
Snow may fall upon you, and gentle springtime rain,
Moon and stars watch over you; so goodbye once again.

When this was demolished a hoard of gold sovereigns was found in the roof.

It was not long before the coming of the Second World War began to make itself felt. In 1935 when it began to be clear that Hitler meant business, Lord Swinton was made Air Minister with the job of building up the RAF as quickly as possible. It had been reduced to a mere skeleton and the industry had seriously declined. However, Lord Swinton did not waste a moment and worked from early morning until late at night. He set up a scheme of shadow factories, ordered Spitfire and Hurricane fighters straight from the drawing board as there was no time for prototypes and established the RAF Volunteer Reserve. There were a number of people who wanted peace and thought that we ought not to prepare for war, and they complained about the work that Lord Swinton was doing at the Air Ministry. Eventually it was decided that the Air Minister ought to be a member of the House of Commons so that he could reply personally to these criticisms rather than the House of Lords and Lord Swinton therefore resigned.

Masham also was beginning to prepare itself and in 1938 Air Raid wardens were appointed, ten for Masham and two in each other parish. Their duty would be to take charge of their areas in the event of an air raid and for this purpose it would be necessary for them to attend a number of lectures which would be given in Masham by instructors appointed by the County Council. First aid points were established at Masham Town Hall and Fearby Institute to deal with minor casualties and as collecting stations for transporting the severely injured to Bedale. As it turned out this was rather a false alarm and arrangements lapsed until the next year.

Dr Cockcroft with members of the Red Cross

However on 4 September 1939 war was declared and life quickly began to change. A Food Control Committee and Local Fuel Advisor were appointed, and children from Gateshead were evacuated into this area. The men from Masham began to join up and go to fight and in many cases die for their country. Those who couldn't, because their jobs were indispensable to the running of the country and the war effort, joined the Home Guard to protect Masham in case of an invasion. Many other soldiers were sent into the area for training purposes. The 12th Company Pioneer Corps were stationed at the Town Hall and billeted in all available accommodation in Masham, and there was also a detachment at Leighton.

During the first winter of the war the weather was so bad that the roads were blocked and Mrs Holland, Commandant of the Red Cross in Masham, remembers that they themselves had to care for all the sick soldiers in the Town Hall and other billets.

The moorland areas were used as training grounds for motor cyclists, small arms firing ranges and artillery ranges. In 1944 there was an air-to-ground firing range on Masham moor. Roomer Common which had been a camp for Roman soldiers some 1700 years before now became a training ground for tanks. Mr Lambert and his family at Nutwith Cote farm were kept awake about four nights a fortnight with tanks and motorcycles driving around most of the night. The farmers had to work especially hard—they were very shorthanded on the farms because as many farmworkers as possible had been called up—and many of them had to do Home Guard work. As well as this they were instructed to plough out old grassland to make the country more self-sufficient in grain. This probably gave some of them a considerable amount of extra work—Tom Pearson remembers what it meant to them on one occasion:

We were visited by two officials from the local War Agriculture Executive Committee one afternoon in the spring of 1940. They had a walk round the fields with my father and requested that we plough out the other half of an eight-acre field in which there was a big old cankered oak tree. This was a big job as there were no mechanical diggers and to get it down we had to dig a trench right round it and chop off all the roots as we came across them. After two good days work we found one morning that it had been blown down during the night. It then had to be sawn up and we had to do this with a cross-cut saw—it was a bit disheartening for a lad of fourteen to saw through an oak tree trunk that is thick enough to almost hide your partner on the other handle. It then had to be taken away in the horse and cart. We had to split up the heavy roots with steel wedges as it was too heavy for our old horse to pull. When we had finally got the tree moved we had to move all the stones that had accumulated on that strip of land, before we could finally plough it.

In 1942 more farm workers were called up and land girls took their place. There were about a dozen in Masham quartered at The Greens.

The Home Guard had its headquarters in the Brewery Yard with an office in Silver Street. Major Watkinson commanded the Masham Home Guard—the following extracts from their papers give an idea of some of their work.

O.C. ALL COMPANIES   11 N.R/39

AID TO CIVIL POLICE IN SEARCH FOR PARACHUTE
OR SEABORNE AGENTS

The following directive has been received from
N.A.S.D. and is forwarded for your information and necessary
action.-

(a)   If the Civil police receive infm that an enemy
agent may have landed by parachute or from the sea,
they may require assistance from Army Units.   In this
event the civil police will contact units (incl. Home Guard)
direct, stating the form of assistance required.

(b)   O&C will endeavour to give the police any assistance
which may be requested.   The responsibility for organising
the search however rests with the Civil police, and units will
as far as possible, carry out the instrs. of the police in
the matter and not initiate separate action.   Any person
detained will immediately be handed over to the civil police.
(c)   Any unit which has taken action at the request of the
police will immediately fwd a report in writing throu h the
usual channels and by the quickest means available to this H. .
setting out the circumstances and the action taken.

(d)   Other units in the vicinity will NOT be infm nor will
any general warning be issued except at the special request
of the Regional Security Liaison officer or on the instrs.
of this Hqrs.

(e)   Although it may, in certain circumstances, be necessary
to circulate fairly widely, the infm that an enemy agent is
believed to be at large, the fact that he (or she) has been
caught, together with his or her name and description and the
circumstances of the arrest remains secret.   If a unit, as a
result of taking action in accordance with the a/m instrs.
comes into possession of such infm, all ranks will immediately
be warned that no mention may be made of the matter in any
circumstances whatsoever.

Leyburn
June 14th 1944

Directive to Home Guard

DIAGRAM F

GERMAN PARACHUTIST, SHOWING TYPICAL UNIFORM AND HARNESS

author of this Handbook has a " hunch " that adolescent enemy agents may be dropped in the uniforms of Boy Scouts or Sea Scouts.

Enemy parachute troops in their own uniform can be recognised quickly from their appearance. A typical German parachutist is shewn in Diagram F. He has high boots laced at the sides, grey loose trousers and tunic with a kind of grey-green overall, gauntlet gloves, a close fitting steel helmet, and a belt to which is attached a revolver or automatic pistol, two haversacks, a water-bottle and a gas-mask. Other equipment is also fastened to him. Any L.D.V. seeing a man or men thus garbed will know what has happened and will act accordingly. But it is well to keep an open and alert mind. Enemy parachutists may be garbed and equipped, if and when they try to land in this country, very differently from when they operated in Holland, Belgium and France. The container, dropped at the end of a separate parachute, may hold: rifle, stick-grenades, anti-tank rifles, machine-guns, heavy or light, ammunition, sticks of dynamite or other explosives for sabotage.

Landings by Sail-planes.—The sail-plane has no engine: its approach will therefore be silent. It can gain height and can be navigated by taking advantage of air currents. It is large and may carry as many as six lightly armed men, or it may

Extracts from Home Guard instruction book

the most practicable method is to put the right knee on the ground and keep the left leg bent, the foot a little in advance of the knee. To achieve steadiness of aim, it is important not to rest on the toes, but to ground both heels firmly.

The prone position gives the most accurate results and the best cover in the open. A variation of it is used in trenches where the parapet is not built up almost vertically with sandbags but is a slope of turf or loose earth. The chief difficulty in the prone position, for beginners, is "getting down to it," and a simple exercise is well worth practising in the garden or on the bedroom carpet. Turn half-right away from the target with the rifle in the loading position. Bend the knees smartly till they touch the ground, the body falling forward. At the same time, grip the rifle firmly with the left hand at the point of balance, release the right hand and drop it, with fingers flat, to take the weight of the body as it falls forward to the ground. The left hand, holding the rifle, should go out almost to its full extent, and it will be found that the butt fits snug with the right shoulder, and the sights can be quickly aligned. The legs should be separated and the feet pressed out and down. It will be found that this movement brings the rifleman flat on the ground, his body slightly at an angle to the line of fire and supported by the legs and belly. The chest and head are slightly

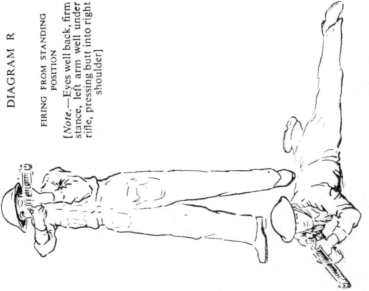

DIAGRAM R

FIRING FROM STANDING POSITION

[*Note.*—Eyes well back, firm stance, left arm well under rifle, pressing butt into right shoulder]

FIRING FROM LYING POSITION

[*Note.*—Eyes well back, left wrist well under rifle, hips flat, legs apart and at angle to direction of fire, heels flat]

maintains continuous fire until the magazine is exhausted. The normal rate is five bursts each of four or five rounds or one magazine a minute. Rapid Fire, or four magazines a minute, is only for emergencies. If the change lever is moved to R (for Rounds) the gun can be fired as a rifle, one round for each trigger pressure: this should be used to economise ammunition or to conceal the presence of a machine-gun. The loading, the stripping (or taking to pieces), and the cleaning of the Bren gun, as well as the quick treatment for stoppages, are best learned under personal instruction, but anyone who has a mental grip of the information given above should in an emergency have a good chance of getting a Bren gun into action (Diagram O).

The Lewis Gun.—This light machine-gun was first put into use during the 1914–18 war and is still an excellent weapon. It is similarly air-cooled, gas-operated and magazine-fed. (Most heavy machine-guns are fed from ammunition belts). The Lewis gun can readily be distinguished from the Bren by the fact that its barrel (which is not interchangeable) is surrounded by a tubular metal case along most of its length. Thus the greater part of the Lewis gun looks like a drain pipe, while the Bren barrel is no thicker than a gas pipe and is bell-shaped at the muzzle. The magazine or drum for the Lewis is disc shaped and fitted

DIAGRAM O

LEWIS GUN

BREN GUN

THOMPSON GUN

Members of the Home Guard

202

HOME GUARD

MASHAM SOUTH Platoon Commander—Lieut. S. W. N. Bedford
Section 1 Sgt Ryder, Cpl T. Lumley, L/C W. A. Jameson, L/C W. Fleetham,
Vols. E. Ellis, H. Fordham, M. Goodburn, F. Holland, J. Holland, F. J. Hunter,
L. S. Hunter, W. H. Hunter, C. l'Anson, A. L. Jackson, G. R. Jackson, J. C.
Jameson, R. C. Kitching.
Section 2 Sgt J. Skirrow, L/C W. T. Lamber, L/C F. Mudd, L/C W. Parratt,
Vols. R. Lamb, G. A. Lattimore, S. Lewis, G. T. Little, G. Mallaby, G. E.
Marshall, W. Marshall, A. V. Mood, W. Moon, R. H. Morris, C. Mudd, E.
Mudd, G. H. Mudd, J. Mudd, D. Nelson, P. Newsome, W. H. Nicholson, E.
Nicholson, A. W. E. Powell, L. Priestley, H. Milner, R. Parker.

MASHAM NORTH Platoon Commander—Lieut F. Pybus
Section 3 Sgt Chrystie, Sgt Theakston, L/C A. Ball, L/C W. E. Bruce, Vols. W.
A. Allinson, H. Allinson, J. A. Bateson, T. W. Beaver, R. W. Bennison, J. Bur-
ton, F. A. Cartwright, F. W. Clark, J. Clark, R. Clark, T. S. Close, A. Coldbeck,
S. J. Coldbeck, R. Croft, C. Clarkson, J. R. Clarkson, J. Birch.
Section 4 Sgt Taylor, Cpl A. Allan, L/C W. G. B. Schofield, R. Scarth, G. C.
Sherwood, L. W. Simms, J. S. Swann, S. Swann, F. J. Taylor, H. A. Thackray,
L. Timms, L. T. Wadsworth, N. Watkinson, J. G. Walker, R. J. Smith, A. H.
Towler.

SWINTON PLATOON Platoon Commander—Capt J. P. Bradford
Section 5 Sgt W. D. Edgar, Cpl H. Burton, L/C N. Binks, L/C R. Pearson, L/C
T. L. Robson, Vols. J. Ascough, J. Banks, J. S. P. Binnington, R. Corps, G.
Harker, J. Harrison, M. Harrison, R. Harrison, A. Jarman, T. Johnson, D.
Kilvington, O. Lambert, H. Nicholson, J. Russell, H. Singleton, J. Stewart, W.
Tennant, G. Thackray, A. Thompson, V. Verity, J. Warren, T. Watson, J.
Wright, P. Young.
Section 6 Sgt G. Thompson, Cpl A. Rough, L/C H. Rider, L/C L. Astwood,
L/C J. Thompson, Vols. H. Barker, A. Coates, G. Coates, J. Coates, B. Collin-
son, C. Collinson, H. Cundall, M. Cundall, V. Cundall, F. Graham, G. Howell,
J. l'Anson, E. Newbould, J. Priestman, J. Simpson, C. Thompson, M. Verity, G.
Pratt, H. Rodney, W. Clark.

ELLINGTON PLATOON Platoon Commander—Lieut G. B. Stubbs
Section 7 Sgt I. Mallaby, L/C A. Croft, L/C A. Roper, L/C H. Clarkson, Vols.
W. Banks, W. Broadley, J. Dawes, J. Ellis, V. Ellis, C. Fox, J. Goodyear, W.
Greensit, G. Hare, D. Middleton, R. Middleton, D. Morris, C. Shaw, E. Shaw, S.
Shaw, H. Thompson, M. Wood.
Section 8 Sgt H. Verity, L/C J. Mawer, Vols. J. Jackson, F. Jackson, J. Jackson,
J. Kingston, H. Mallaby, J. Thompson, J. Vollans, E. Walker, R. Wilson, G.
Pratt, H. Rodney.

White Bear Hotel

They had observation posts at Leighton Bank, Roomer and Sail Hill. They had to patrol and search the moors and woods in case of invasion, to search for parachute troops or spies being dropped. On the night of 16 April 1941 the war came right into Masham. Soon after dark a terrific explosion was heard all over the town. Two parachute mines had landed on the White Bear Hotel. Things were thrown around in all the houses nearby. Six people were killed and a number of buildings including the White Bear were demolished.

There were also firewatchers organised by Mr Brown, the fire guard officer. They took turns watching for fires from the church steeple. The scouts collected waste paper and scrap iron was also collected. Later in the war munition shelters were put up along the roadsides and in some fields to house the ammunition needed on the Second Front. There were over 800 in the immediate vicinity of Masham. Masham station was kept open seven days a week with the help of the military to dispatch the ammunition. In the few weeks before D-Day, up to forty special trains were sent out of Tanfield.

At Swinton like everywhere else in the district the coming of the war changed things. When war was declared Sir Winston Churchill asked Lord Swinton to preside over the board of leading businessmen who prevented the Germans from obtaining many important war supplies and also over the Security Executive dealing with security in this country and overseas. As a result he was placed at the head of Hitler's list for 'liquidation' when the Nazis captured Britain. In 1942 he was sent as Resident Minister to West Africa to ensure an adequate supply of the essential supplies such as fats, and bauxite that came from there. Lady Swinton joined the ATS and worked at Richmond interviewing recruits. Mr John Cunliffe-Lister joined the army and was never to return to Masham as he was killed while fighting in North Africa. Mr Philip Cunliffe-Lister joined the RAF and won an MC. Swinton itself was taken over by Harrogate College with some of the staff living at Glebe House, and the Old Vicarage was the sick bay. The air raid shelter behind the Old Vicarage was put there for these children and more were built in the sunken wall round the garden at Swinton. The estate was run on a skeleton staff, as all those who could be spared joined up.

War memorial in Masham churchyard

The end of the war saw the beginning of the greatest change to farming—the widespread coming of tractors and mechanisation. Unfortunately, their coming was not without tragedy—a youth of 21 was killed during the war at Ilton when his tractor overturned and burst into flames. Most of the district now had electricity and life became more as we now know it. With more mechanisation there was less employment on the land and the villages became smaller. Masham itself expanded with the building of new council houses on the Leyburn Road, but the rest of the town changed very little.

(from left to right) The Rt. Hon. Reginald Maudling, the Rt. Hon. Edward Heath and Lord Swinton walking in the grounds at Swinton

After the war when Harrogate College left Swinton, Lord Swinton offered it to the Conservative Party and they established a college there. For many years it was visited by all the leading members of the party as well as rank and file members from all over the country.

The beautiful situation and grounds were much appreciated by all those who came. William Danby can little have realised 150 years before when he laid out the grounds and planted the shrubs and trees how many people would come to stay at Swinton and walk round and appreciate his work. Lord and Lady Swinton continued to live in the central part of the house surrounded by the many lovely paintings and pieces of furniture which had been collected by the owners of Swinton over many years. After the war Lord Swinton was made Minister for Civil Aviation before Labour came into power and in 1951 he became Chancellor of the Duchy of Lancaster and Minister of Materials and then served as Commonwealth Relations Secretary for three years.

Over the centuries, as we have seen, the Lords of Mashamshire and latterly the owners of Swinton estate have had a lot of influence over the lives of those who live in Mashamshire, in recent years mostly in country districts. Swinton estate was lucky in that for fifty years from 1924–74, which included many difficult times, it was owned by someone who thought more about the welfare and wellbeing of her tenants than her own financial gain. Tom Pearson remembers her in the following words:

> Our lady, as she was often referred to, was a well respected, loved and admired figure in our midst, knowing each of her eighty-four farmer tenants individually by christian names, in my case knowing my father before me and my grandfather before him. This applies to most other tenants on the estate as well. The fact that we sons have been able to take over the tenacy of a farm after our fathers has helped to build up a wonderful and happy relationship between landlord and tenant.

With the death of Lord Swinton in 1972 and Lady Swinton in 1974 Mashamshire lost two very good friends and one feels an era has come to an end. I feel that this is a sad but suitable note on which to end this chronicle of Mashamshire and I hope that whoever writes the next chapter will find that although things have progressed, it will not have changed from the happy place it now is.

The coffin lake at Swinton

References

Chapter One
1 Field names of Mashamshire 1800
2 Yorkshire Archaeological Journal
3 Fisher's History of Masham
4 Wade's Causeway

Chapter Two
1 Roman Roads—Margary
2 Ripon Millenium
3 Fisher's History of Masham
4 Archaeological Register at County Hall, Northallerton
5 Field names of Mashamshire 1800
6 Field names of Mashamshire 1800
7 Place names of the North Riding, A. H. Smith

Chapter Three
1 Fisher's History of Masham
2 Place names of the North Riding, A. H. Smith
3 Place names of the North Riding, A. H. Smith
4 Fisher's History of Masham

Chapter Four
1 Fisher's History of Masham
2 Place names of the North Riding, A. H. Smith
3 Fisher's History of Masham

Chapter Five
1 Fisher's History of Masham
2 Fisher's History of Masham
3 Fisher's History of Masham

Chapter Six
1 Swinton papers at County Hall, Northallerton
2 Masham papers at Trinity College, Cambridge
3 Fisher's History of Masham

Chapter Seven
1 Fisher's History of Masham
2 Swinton papers at County Hall, Northallerton

Chapter Eight
1 Fisher's History of Masham
2 Chartulary of Fountains
3 Chartulary of Fountains

Chapter Nine
1 Cunliffe-Lister papers at Bradford City Library*
2 Swinton papers at County Hall, Northallerton

Chapter Ten
1 Cunliffe-Lister papers at Bradford City Library
2 Fisher's History of Masham
3 Cunliffe-Lister papers at Bradford City Library
4 Fisher's History of Masham
5 Fisher's History of Masham
6 Cunliffe-Lister papers at Bradford City Library

Chapter Eleven
 1 The original belonged to J. E. Whiting, Esq., now in amenity Library, Leeds
 2 Cunliffe-Lister papers at Bradford City Library
 3 Swinton papers at County Hall, Northallerton
 4 Cunliffe-Lister papers at Bradford City Library
 5 Masham papers at Trinity College, Cambridge
 6 Swinton papers at County Hall, Northallerton
 7 Fisher's History of Masham
 8 Swinton papers at County Hall, Northallerton
 9 The Pennine Dales by A. Raistrick
10 Swinton papers at County Hall, Northallerton
11 Cunliffe-Lister papers at Bradford City Library
12 Cunliffe-Lister papers at Bradford City Library

Chapter Twelve
1 Julius Caesar Ibbetson by Rotha Mary Clay
2 William Jackson's biography
3 The 1851 census at County Hall, Northallerton
4 Cunliffe-Lister papers at Bradford City Library

* Now at County Hall, Northallerton

210

Index